Olga Goloveshkina

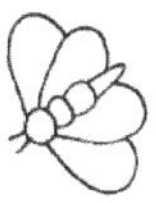

# Fox travel

COLORING BOOK

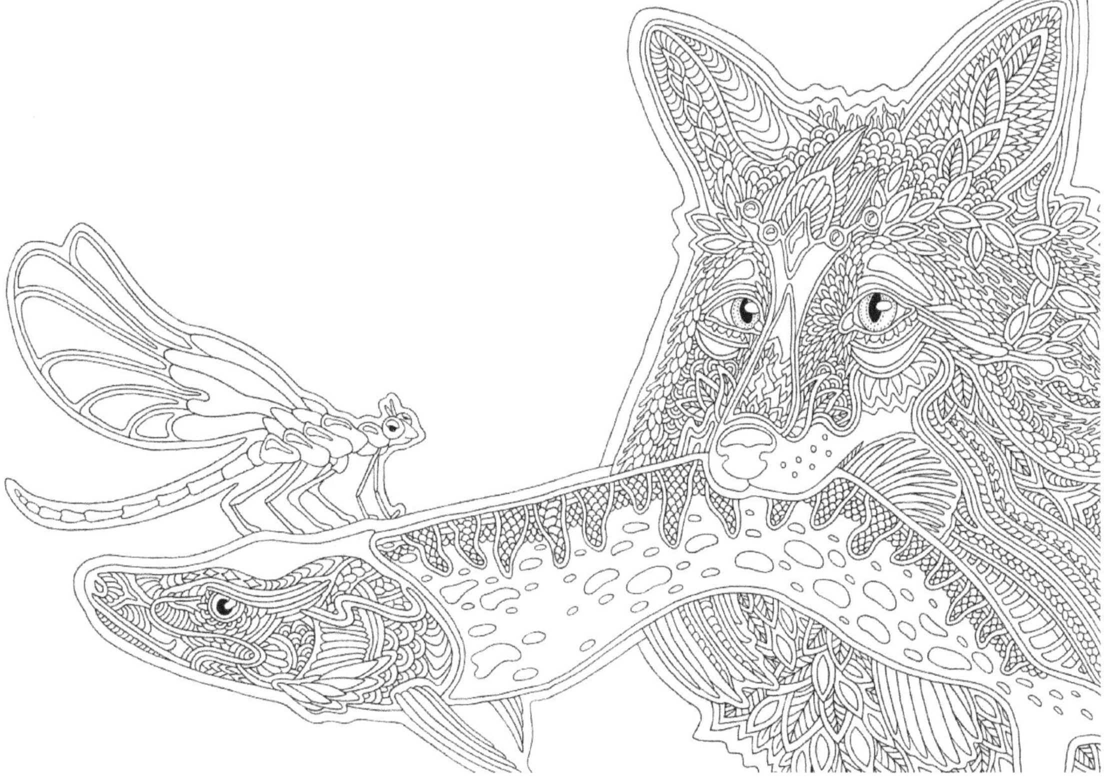

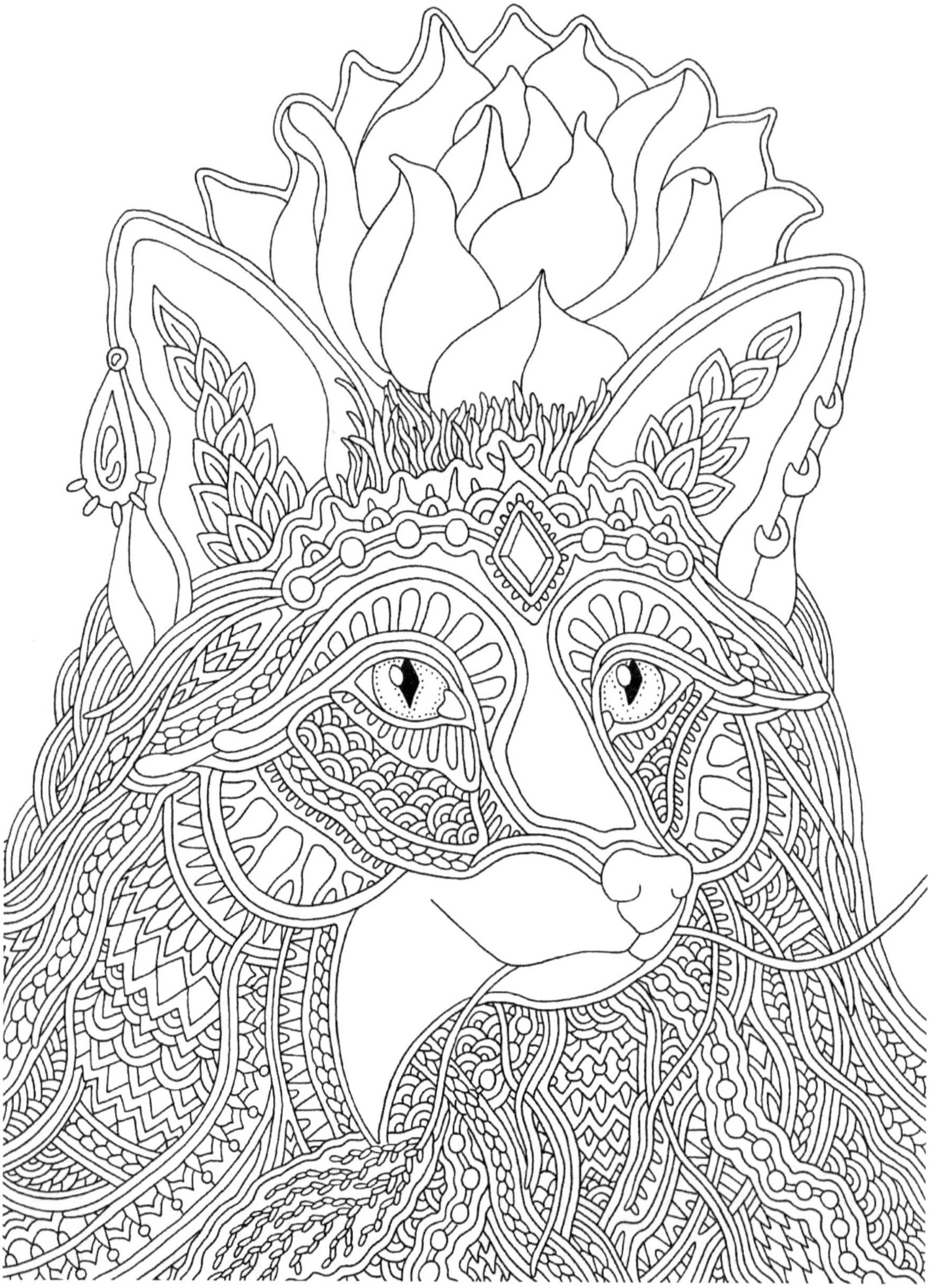

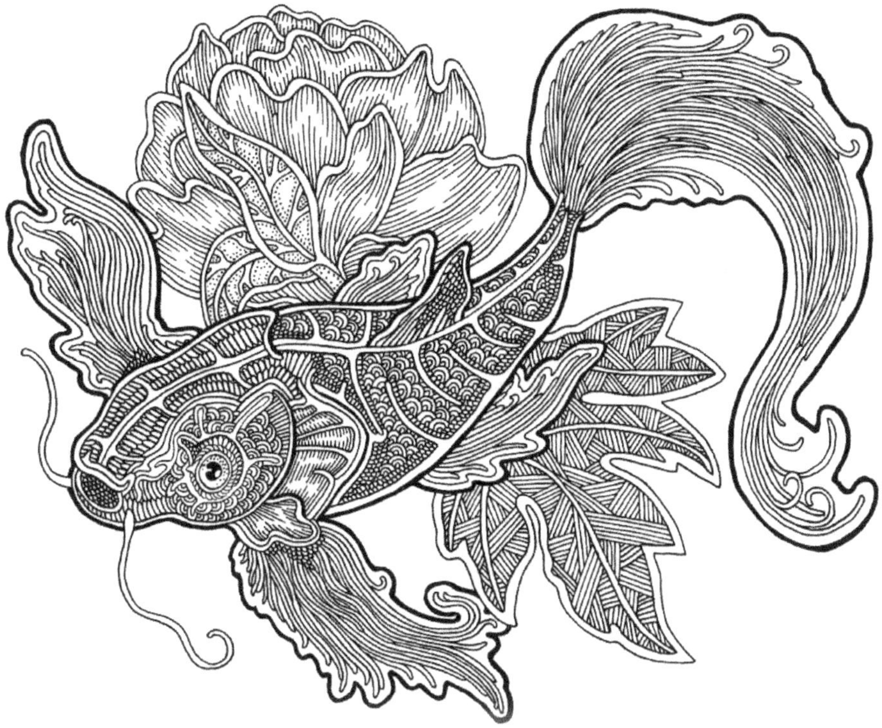

This book belongs to

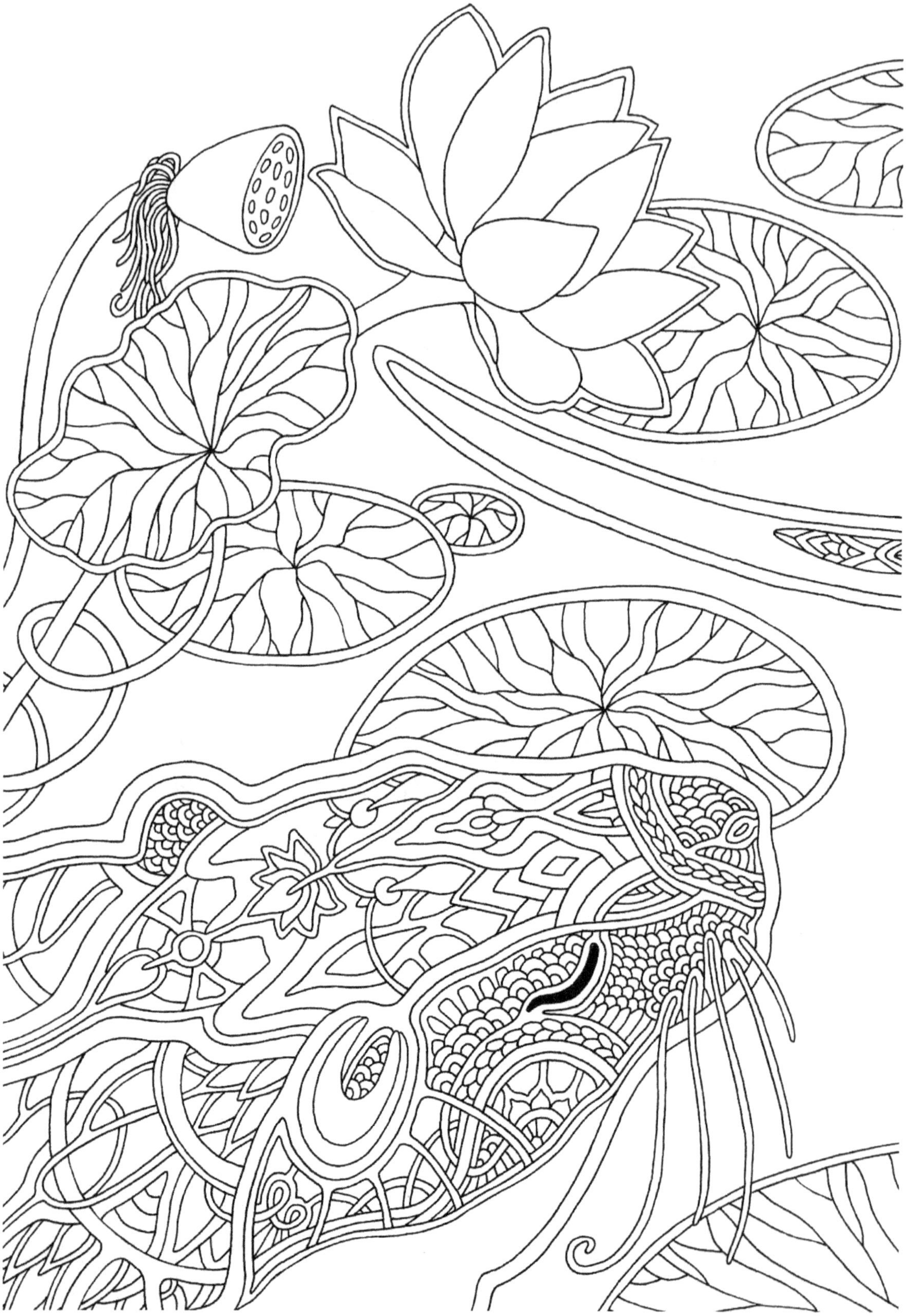

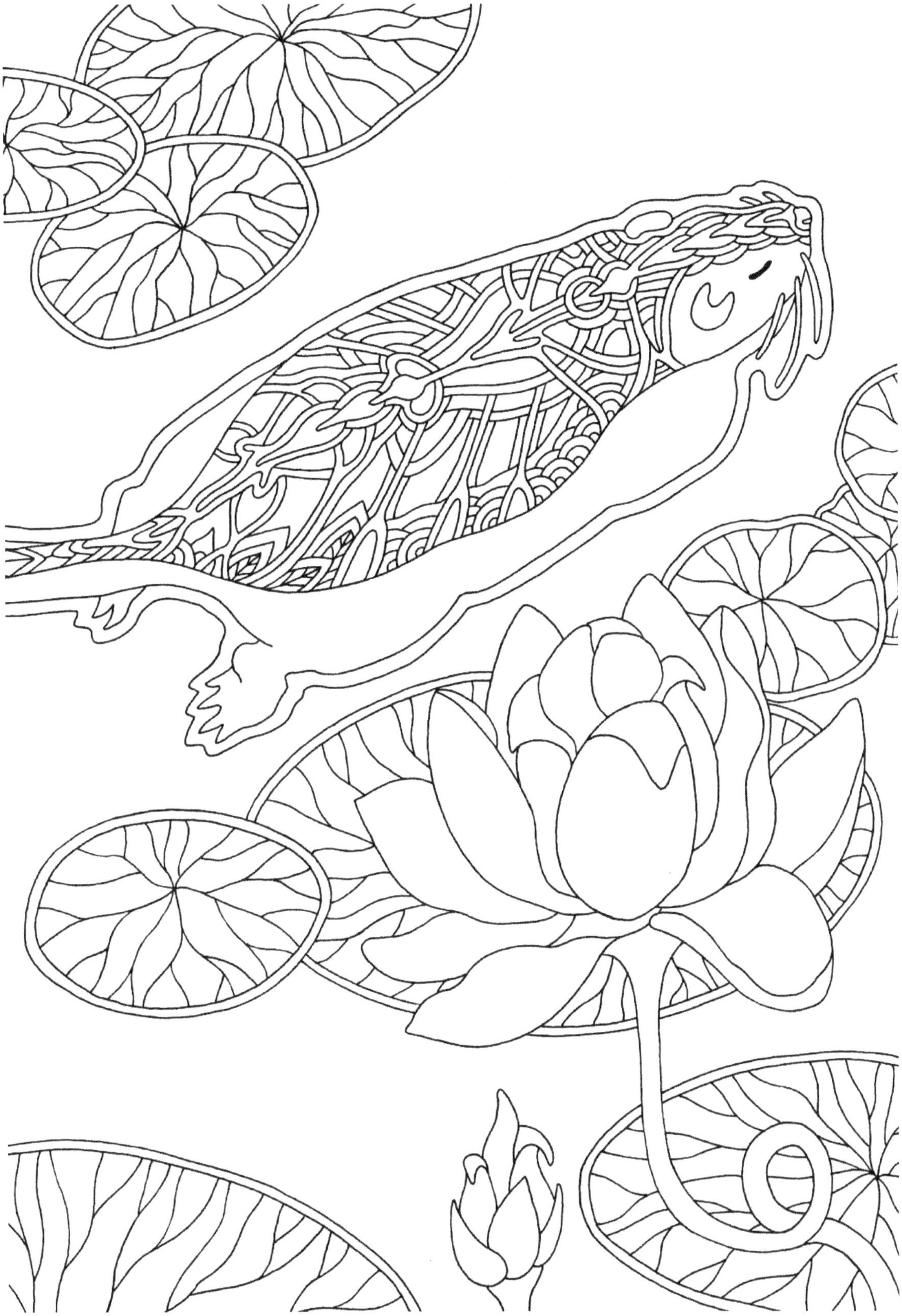

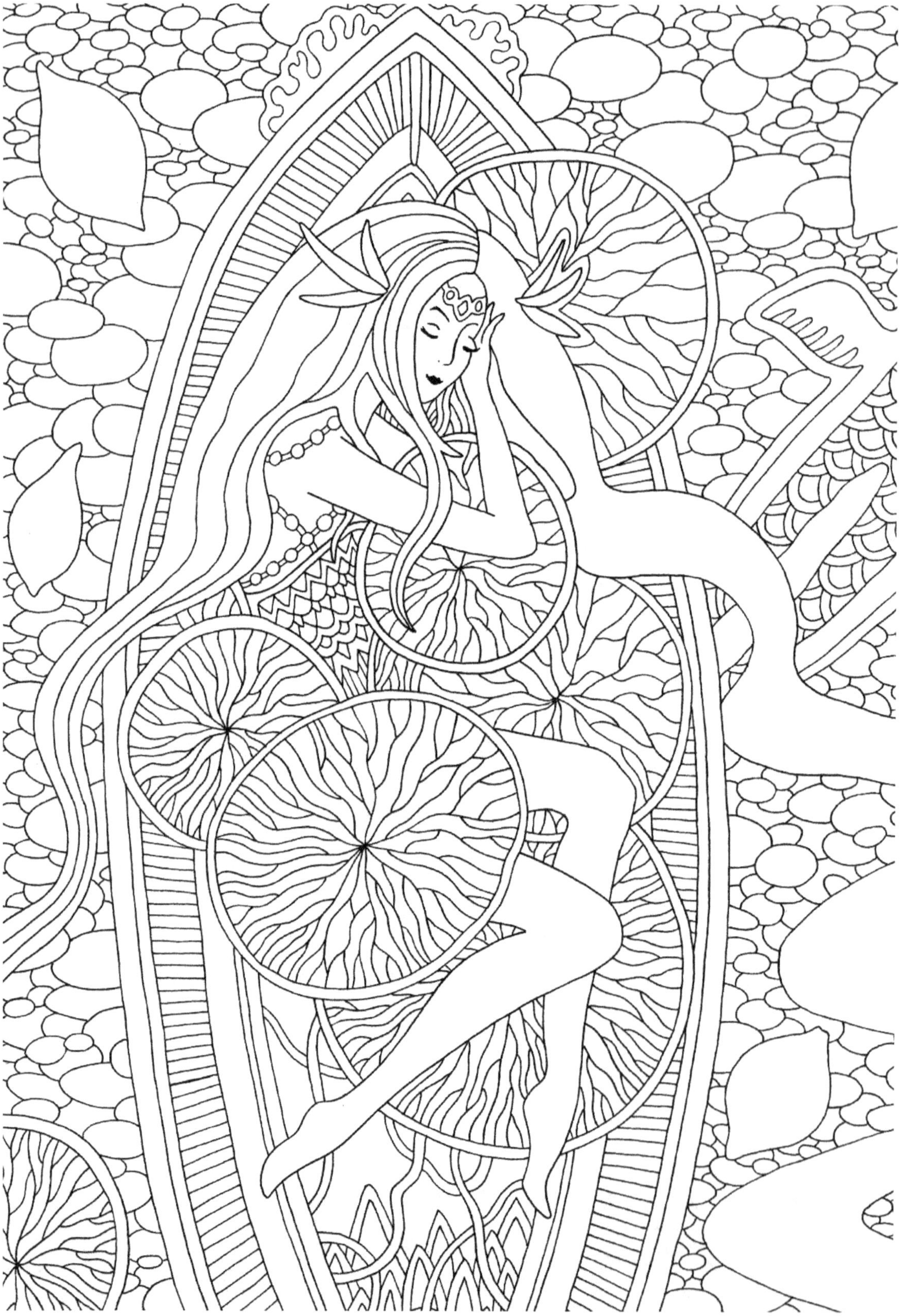

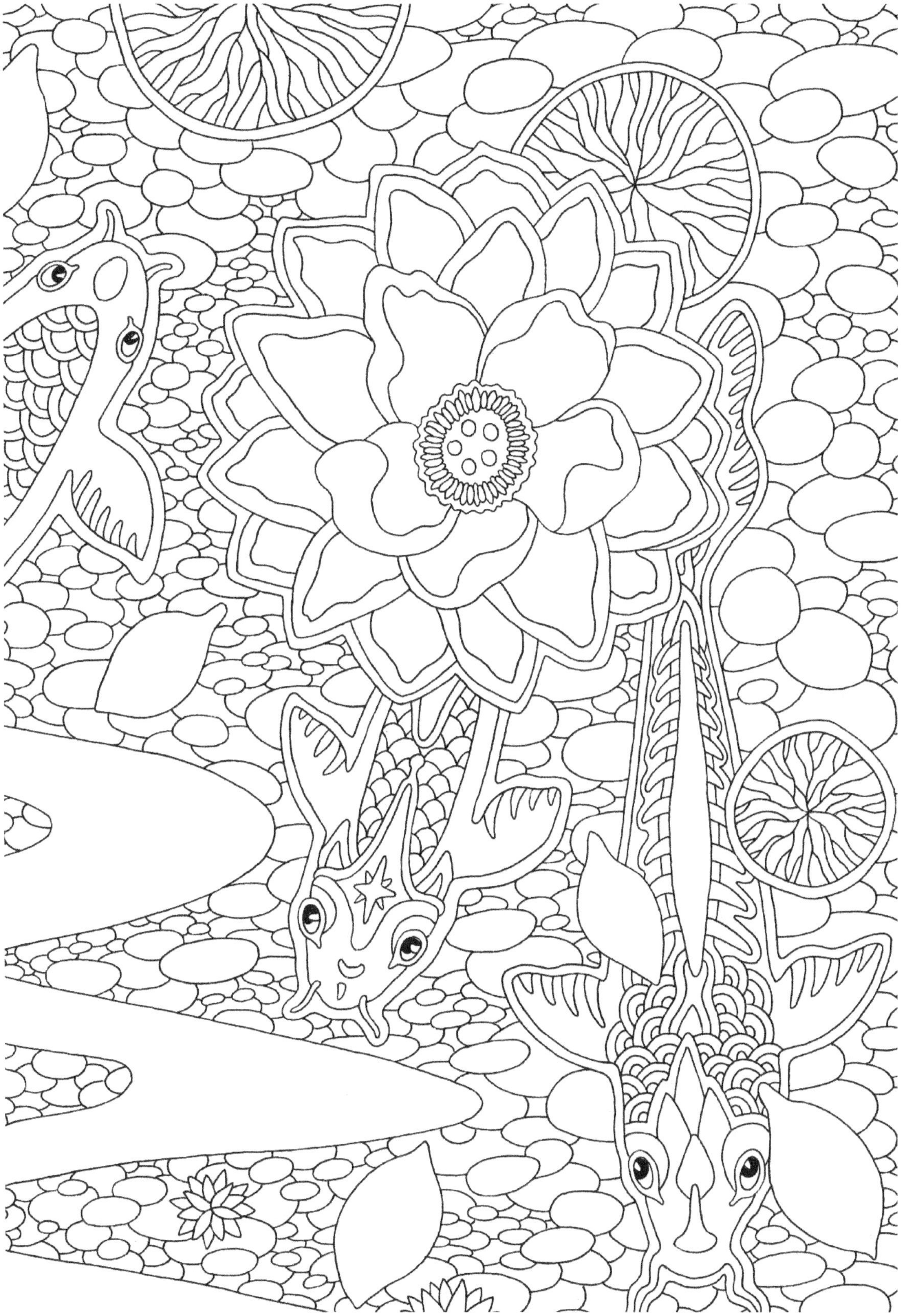

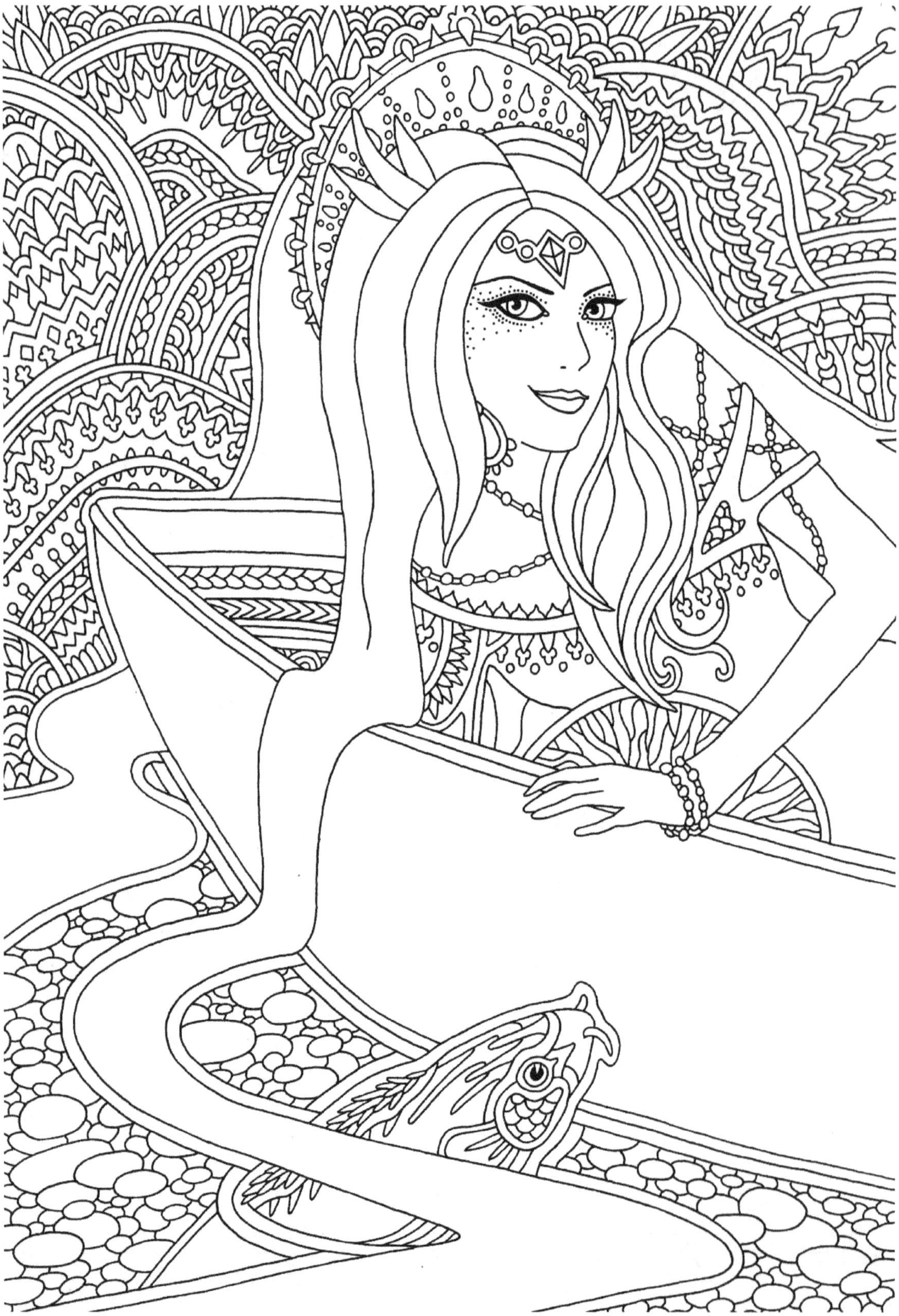

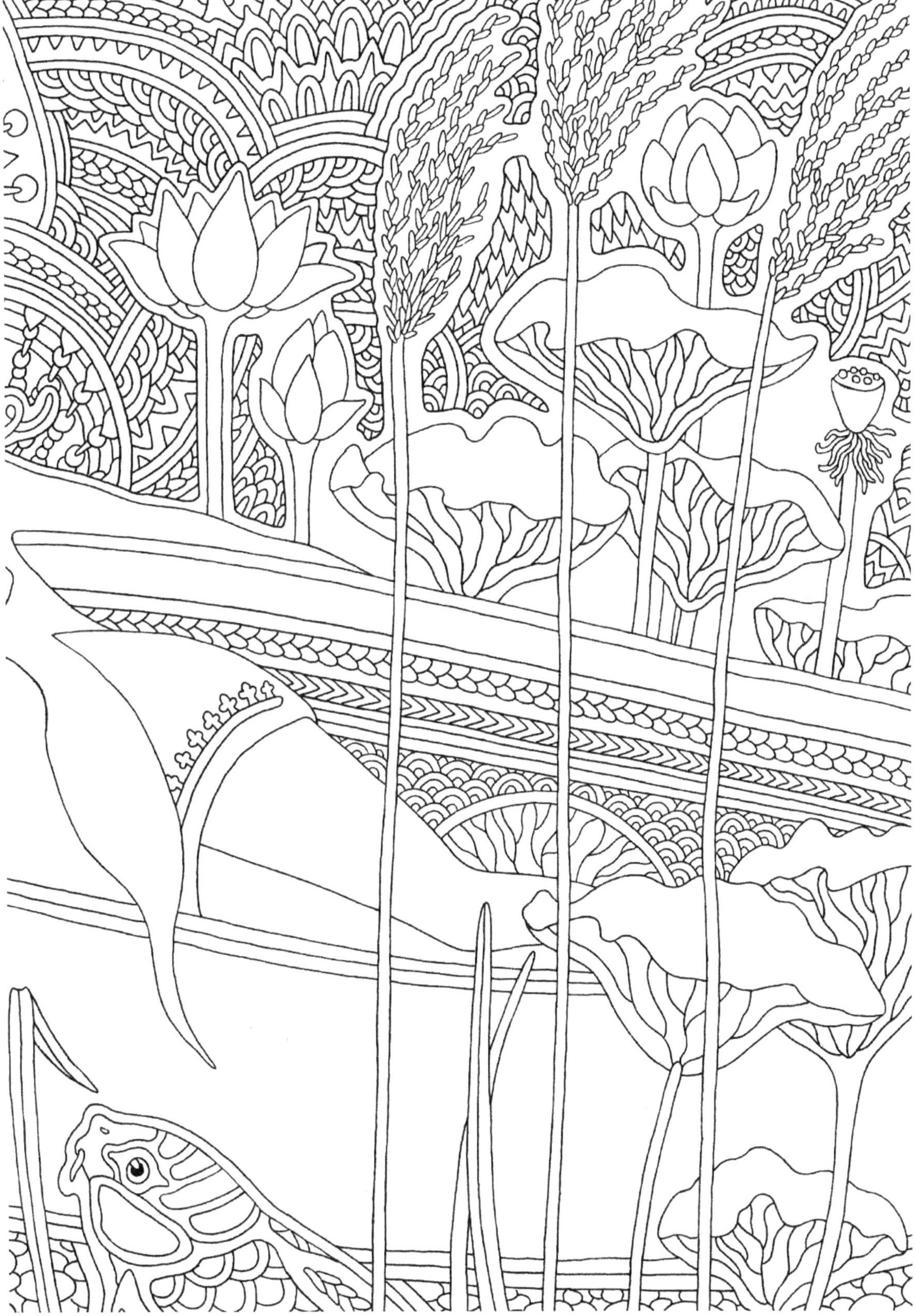

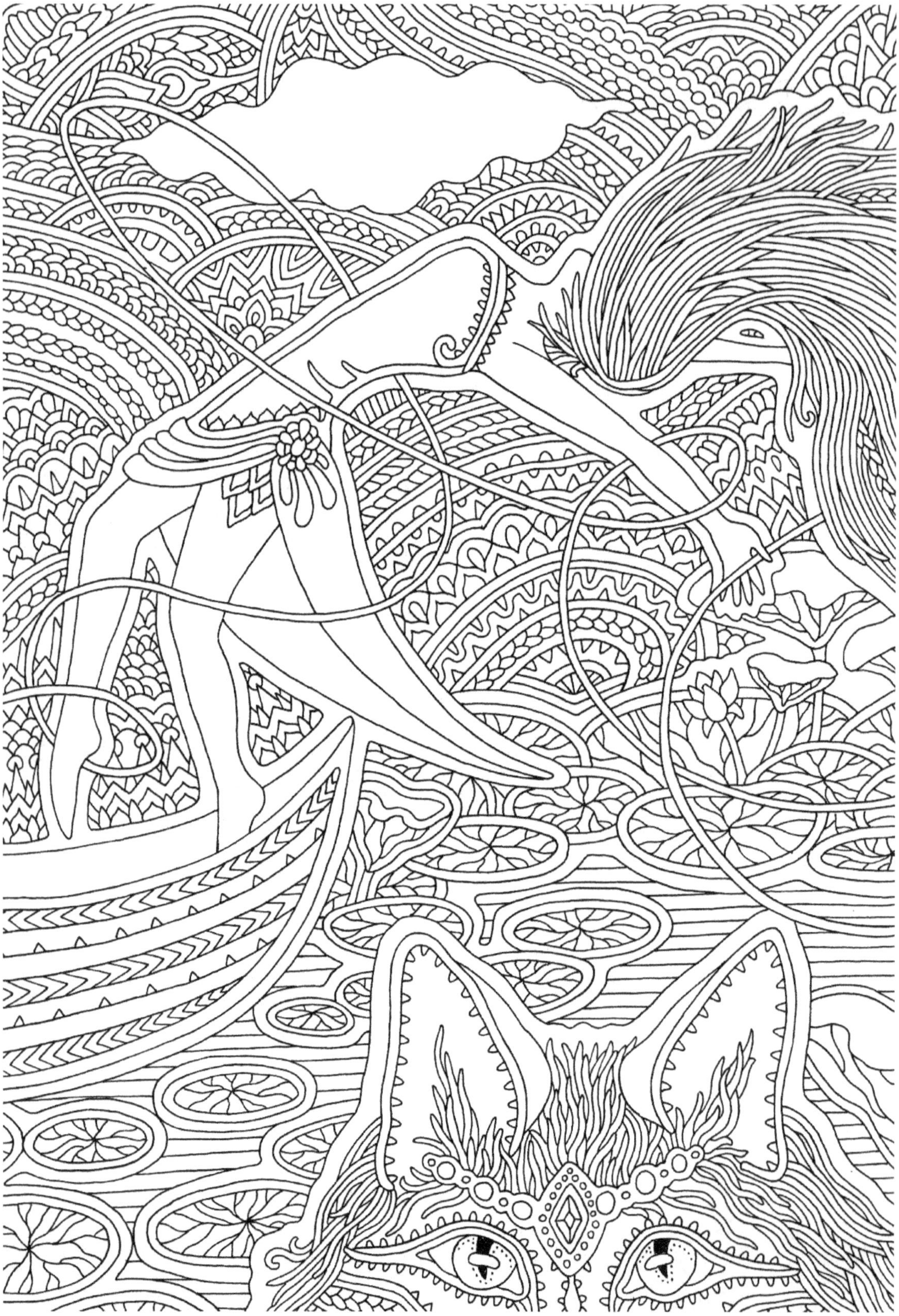

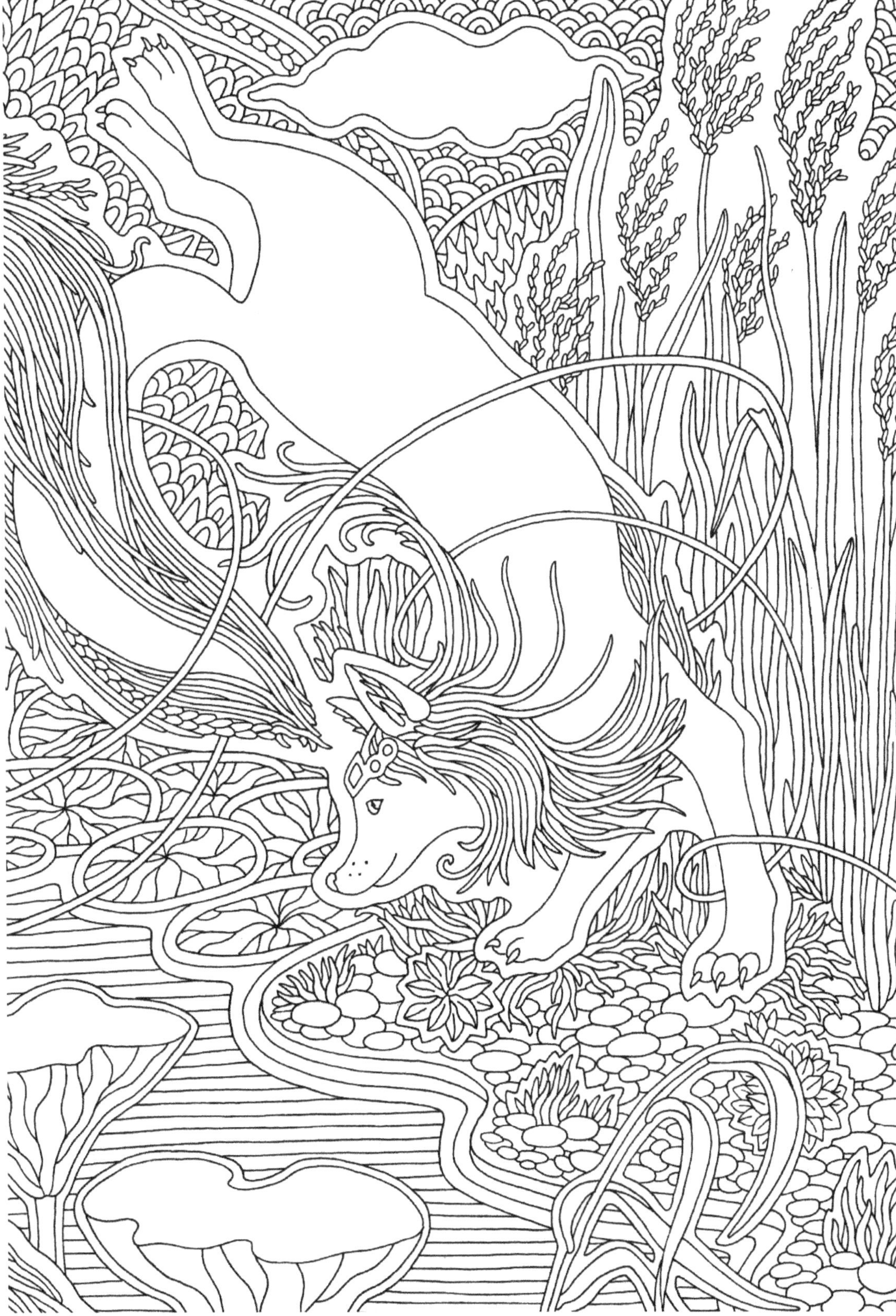

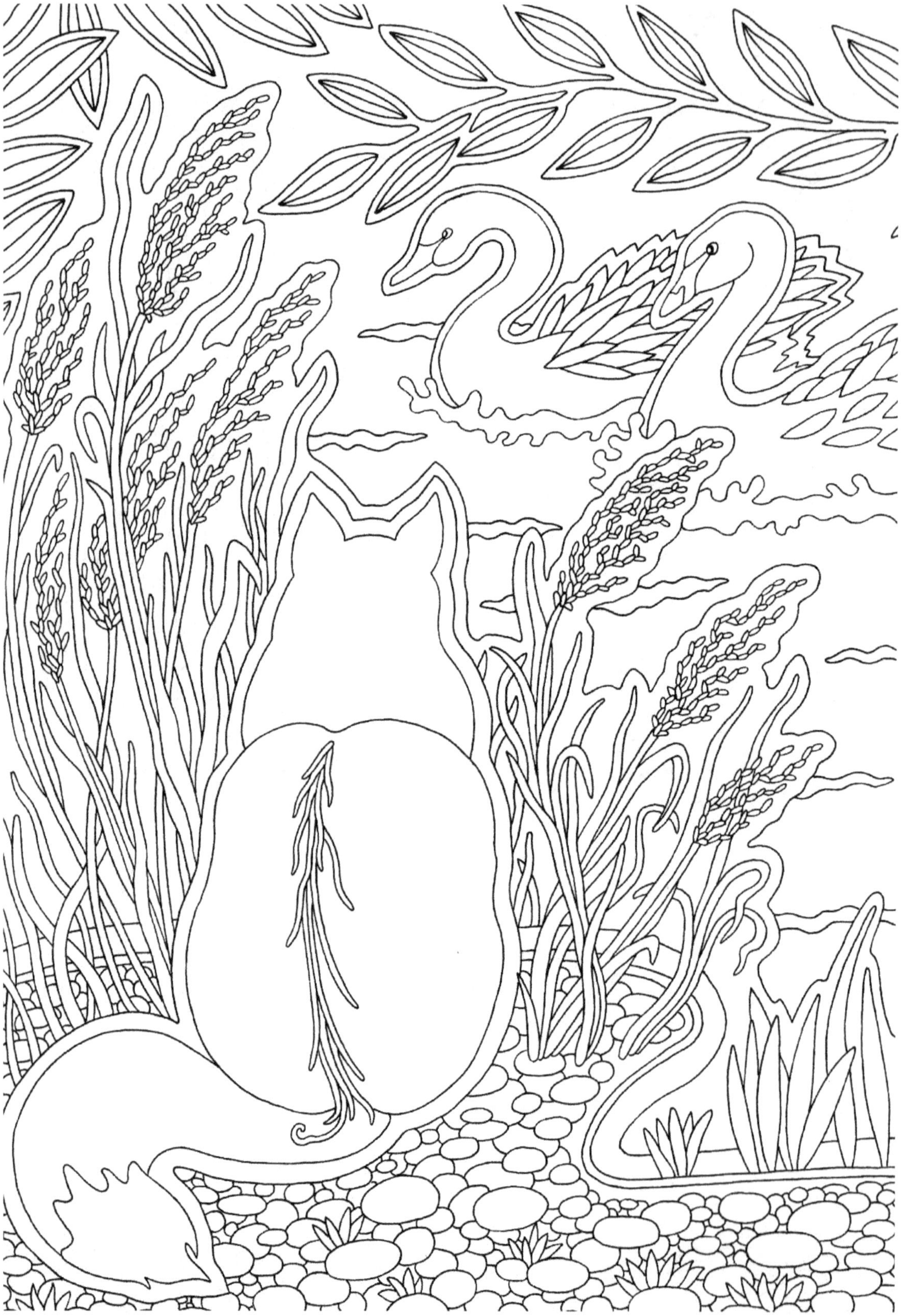

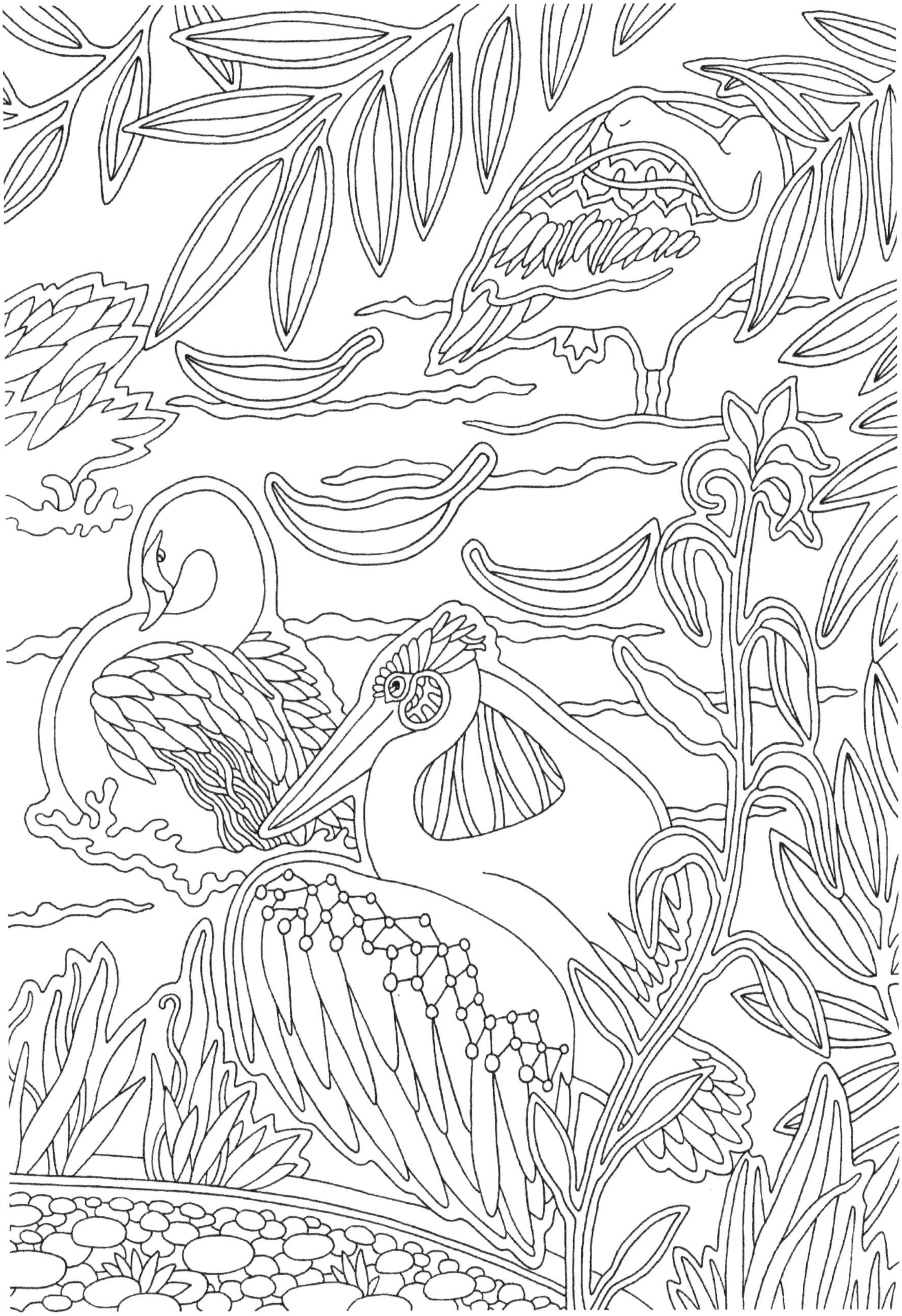

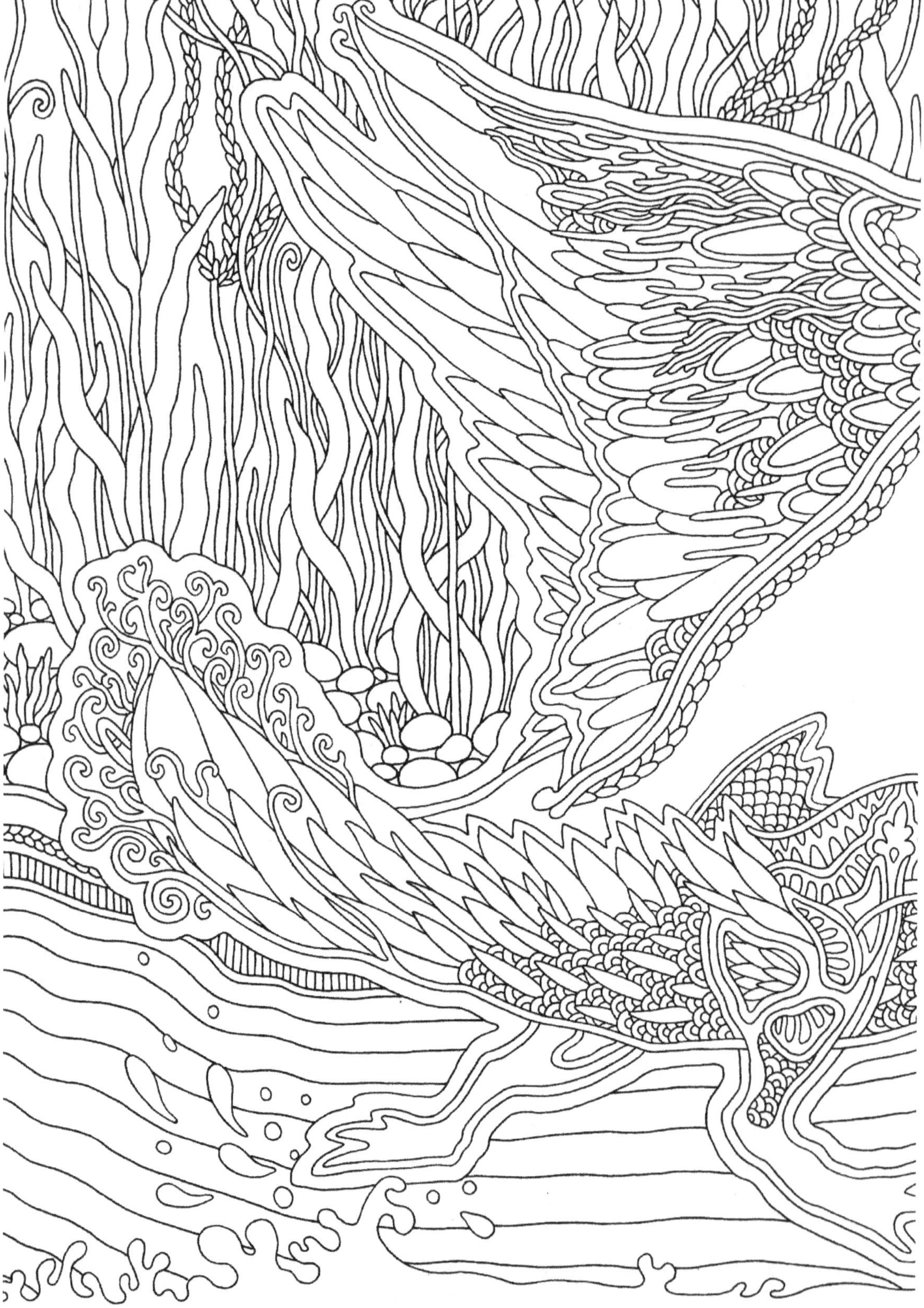

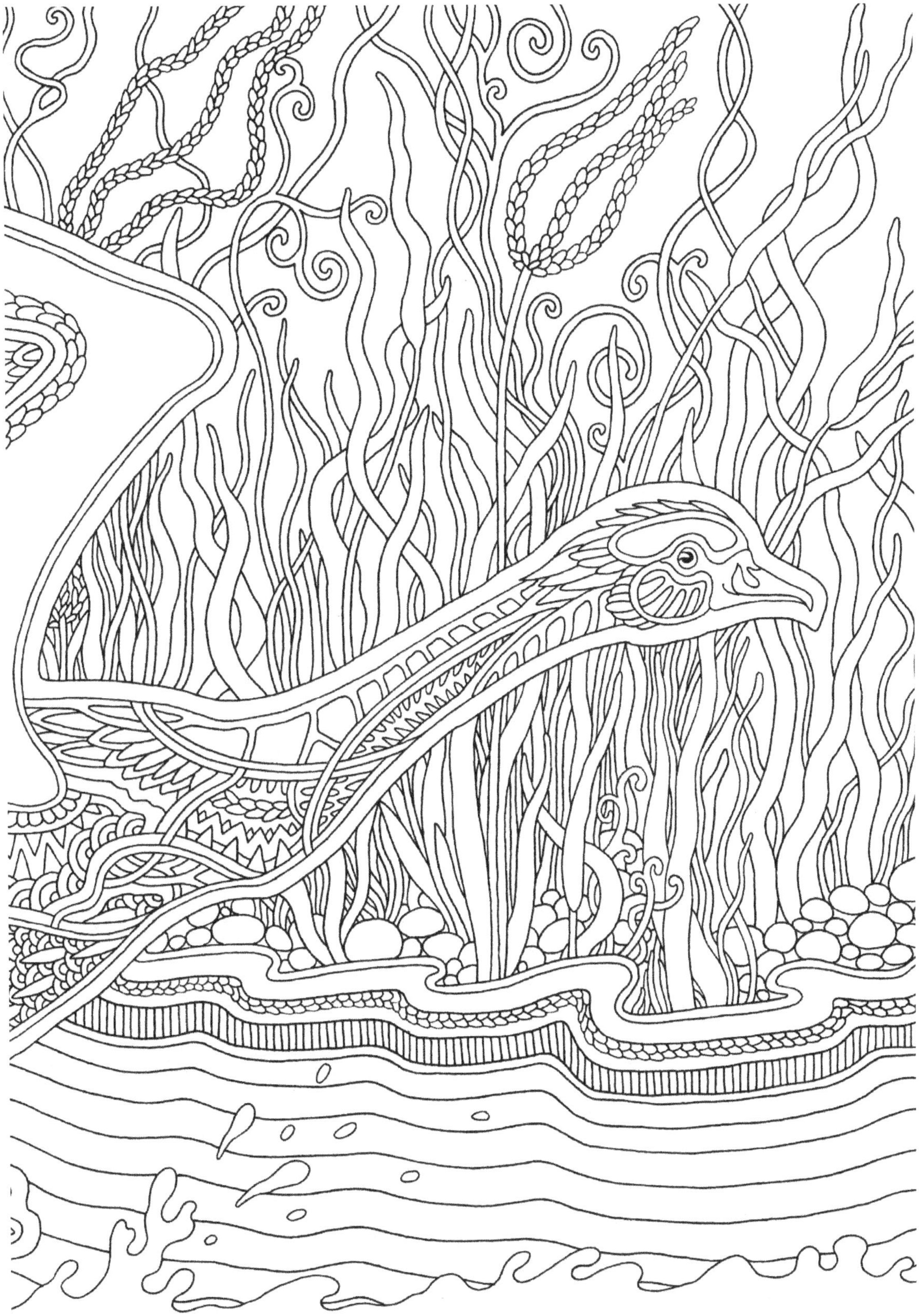

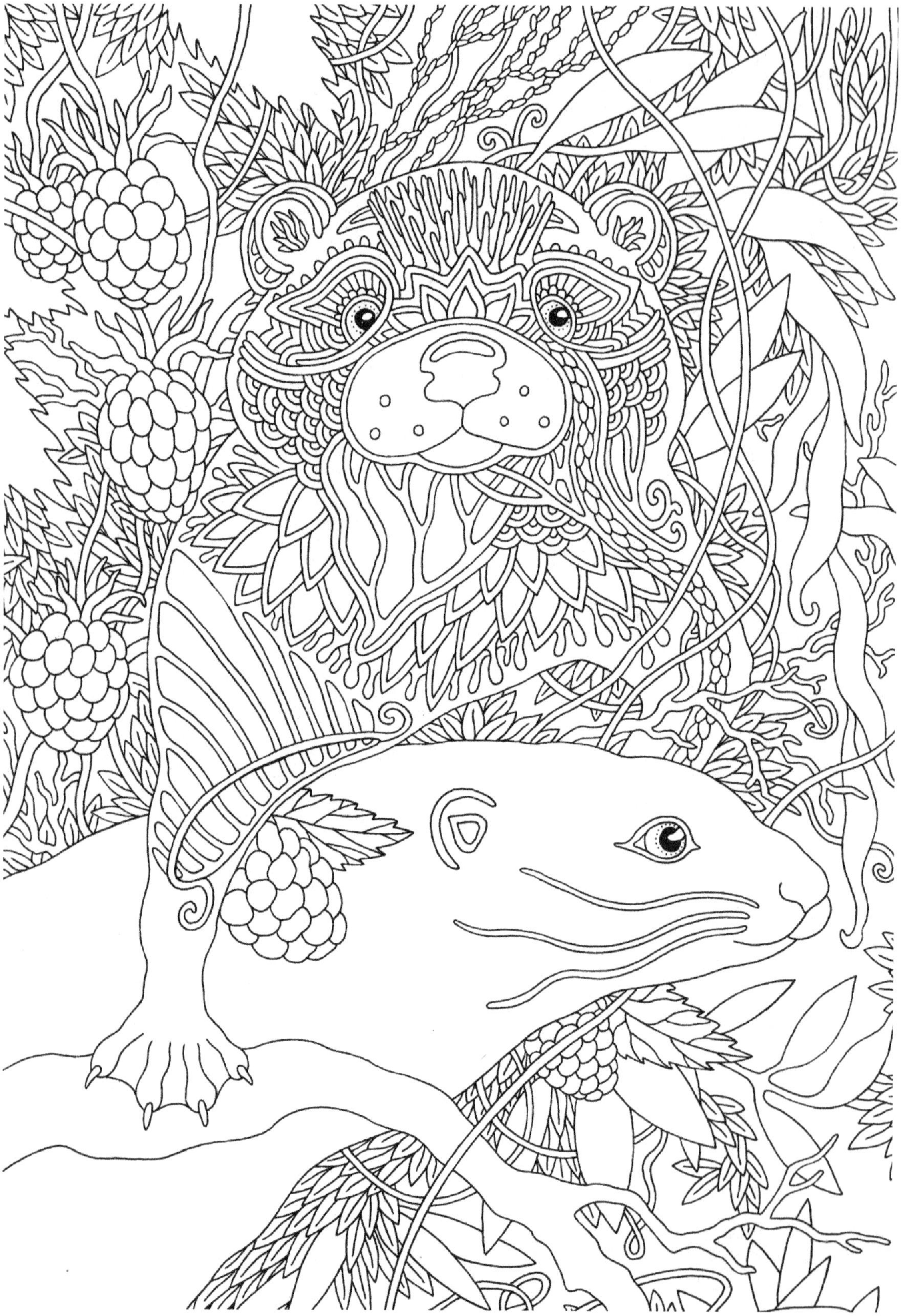

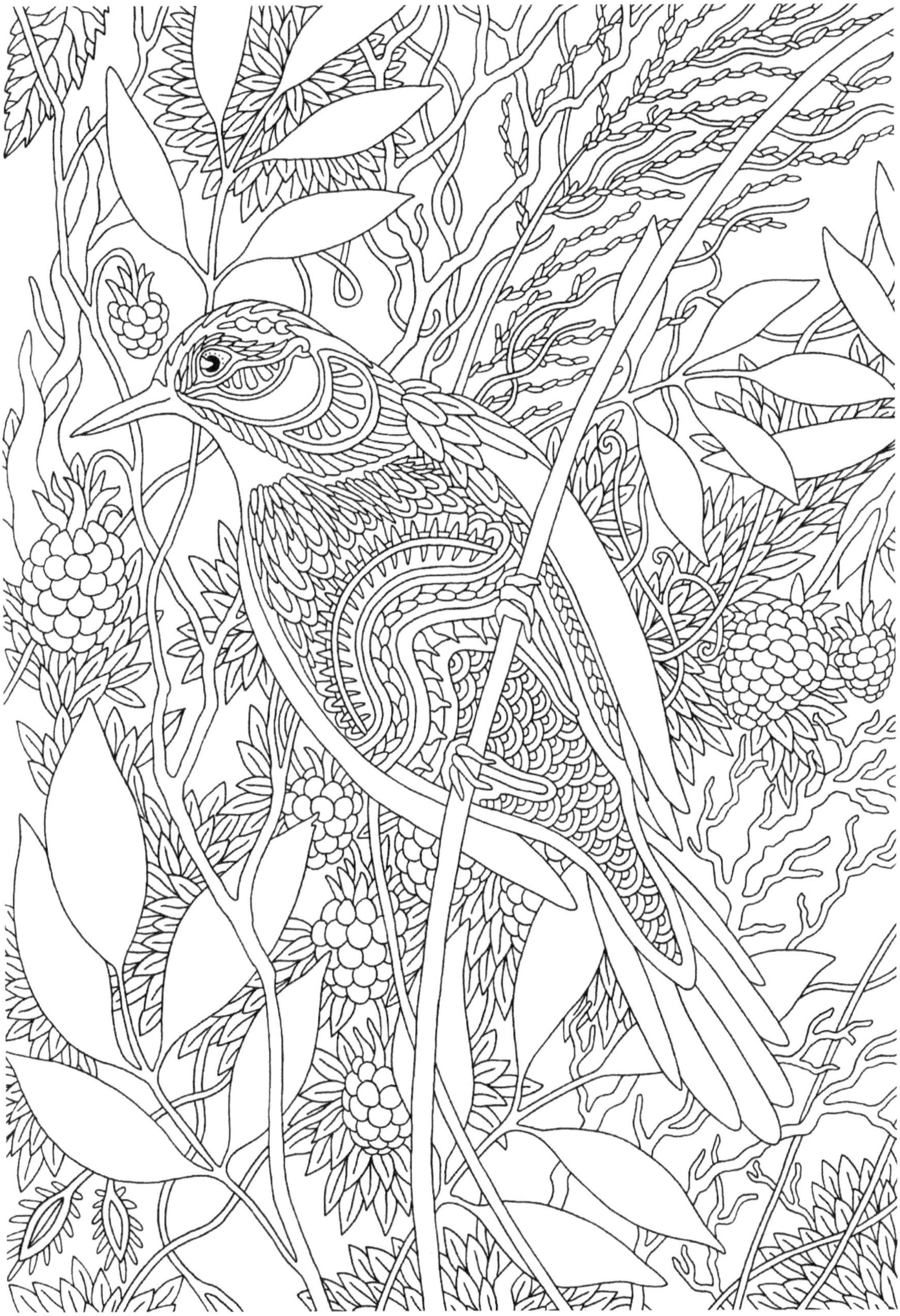

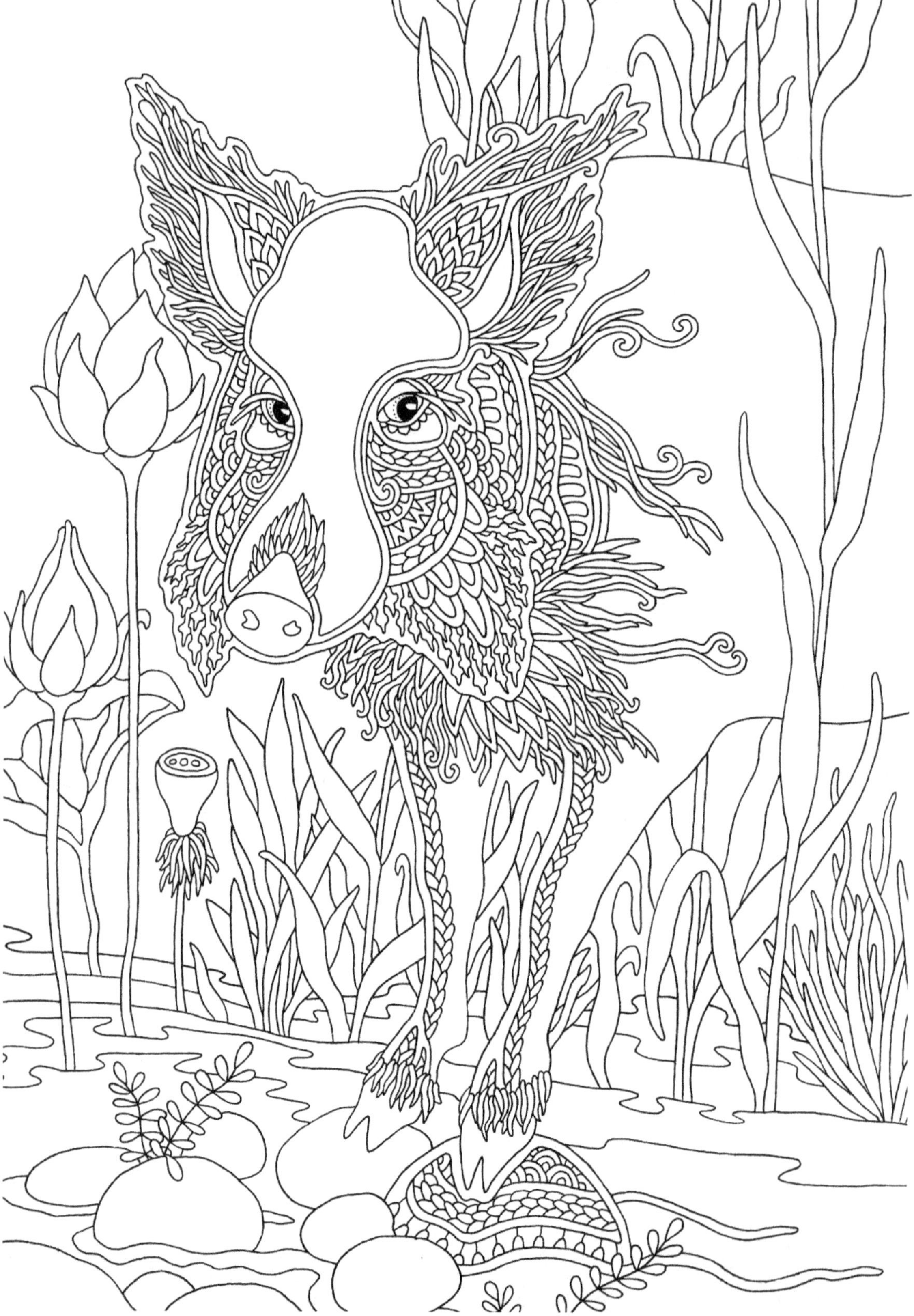

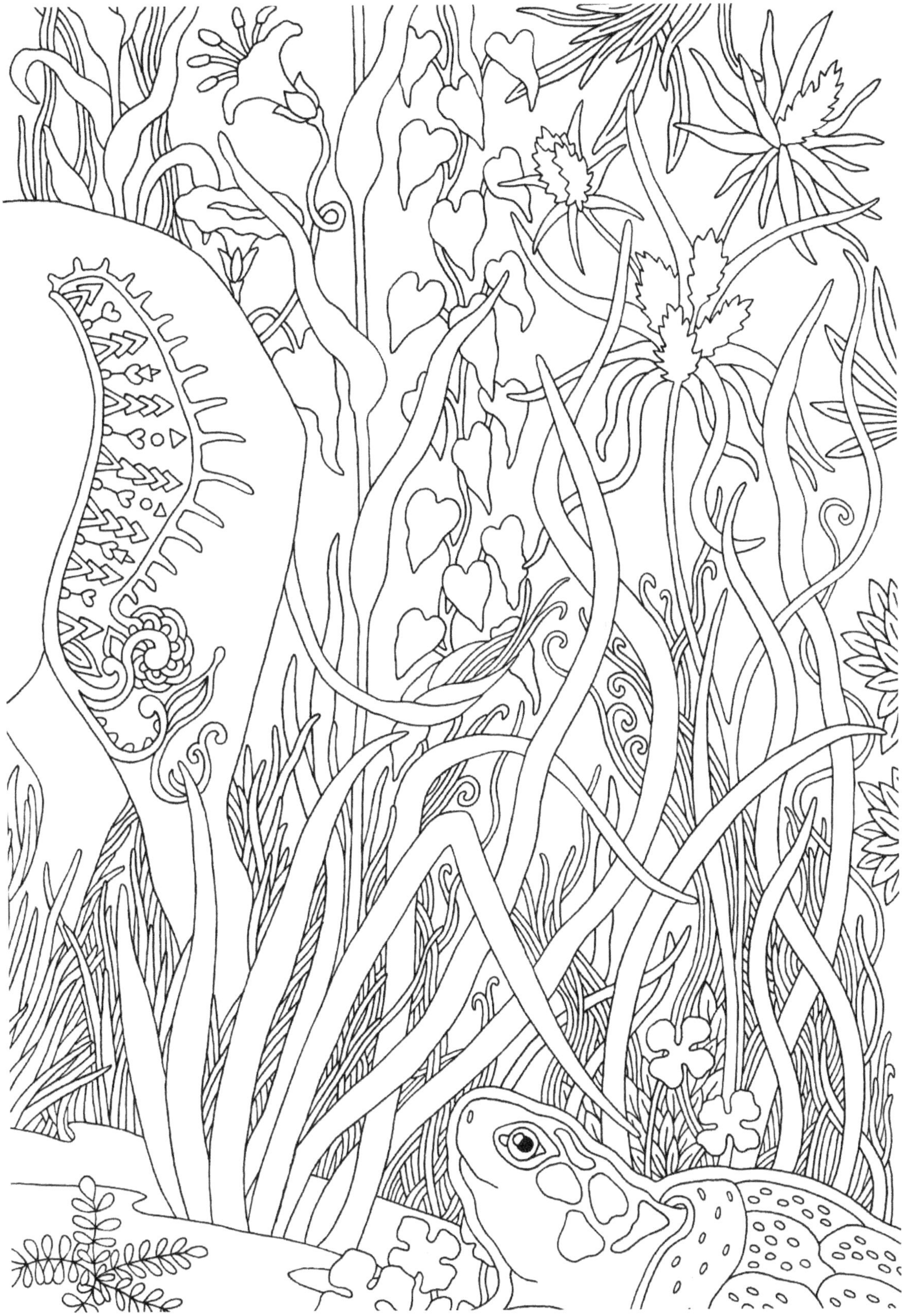

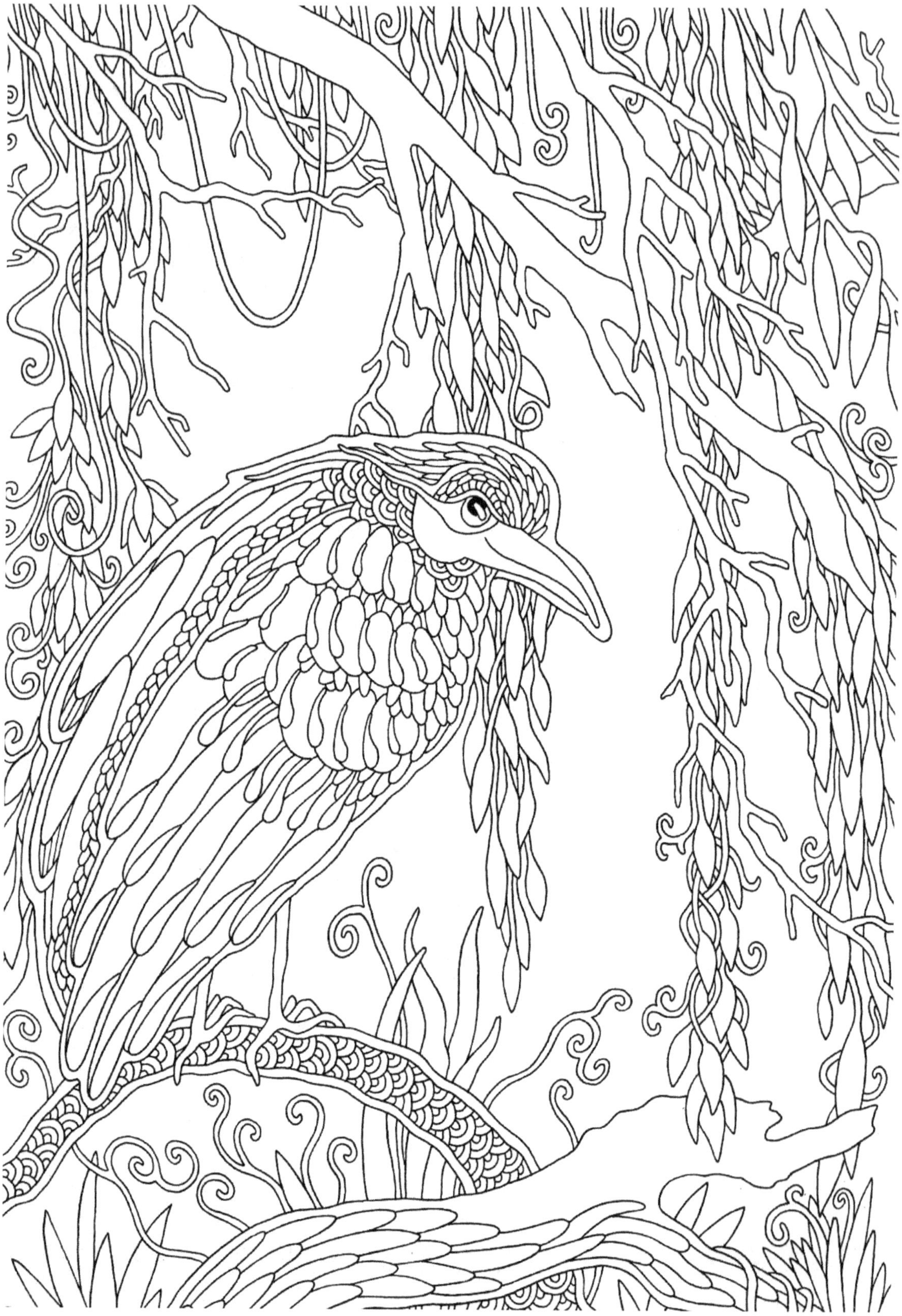

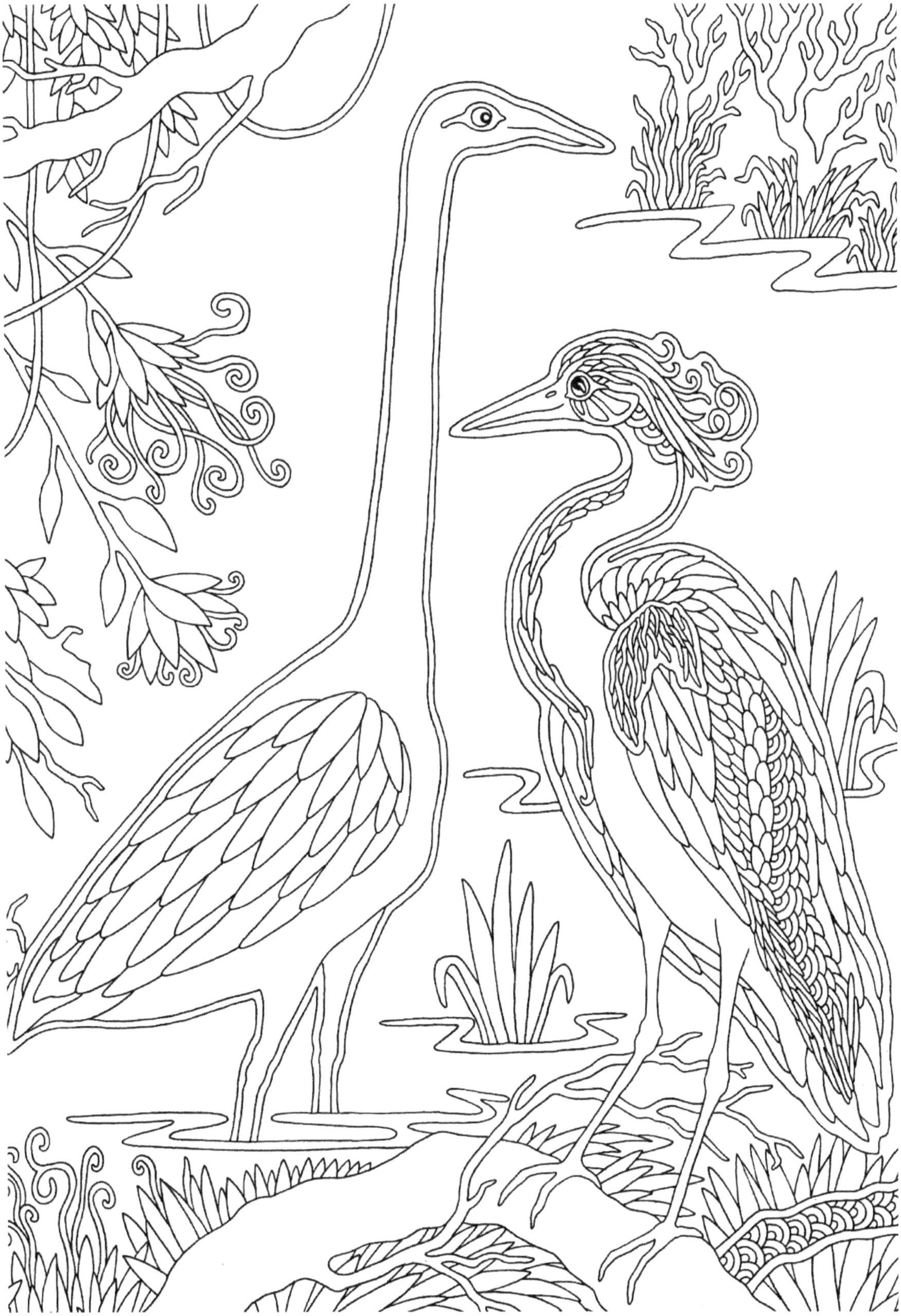

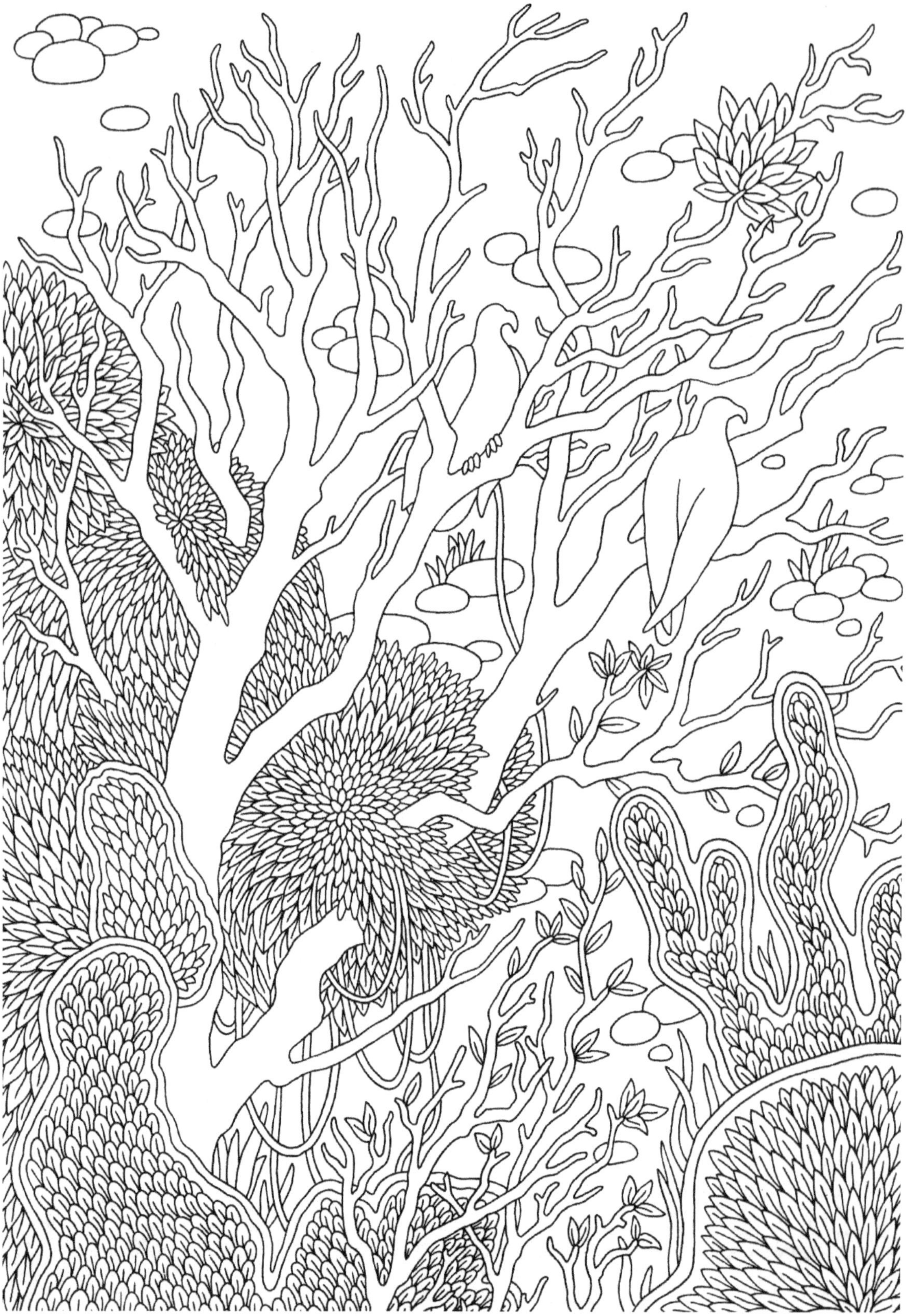

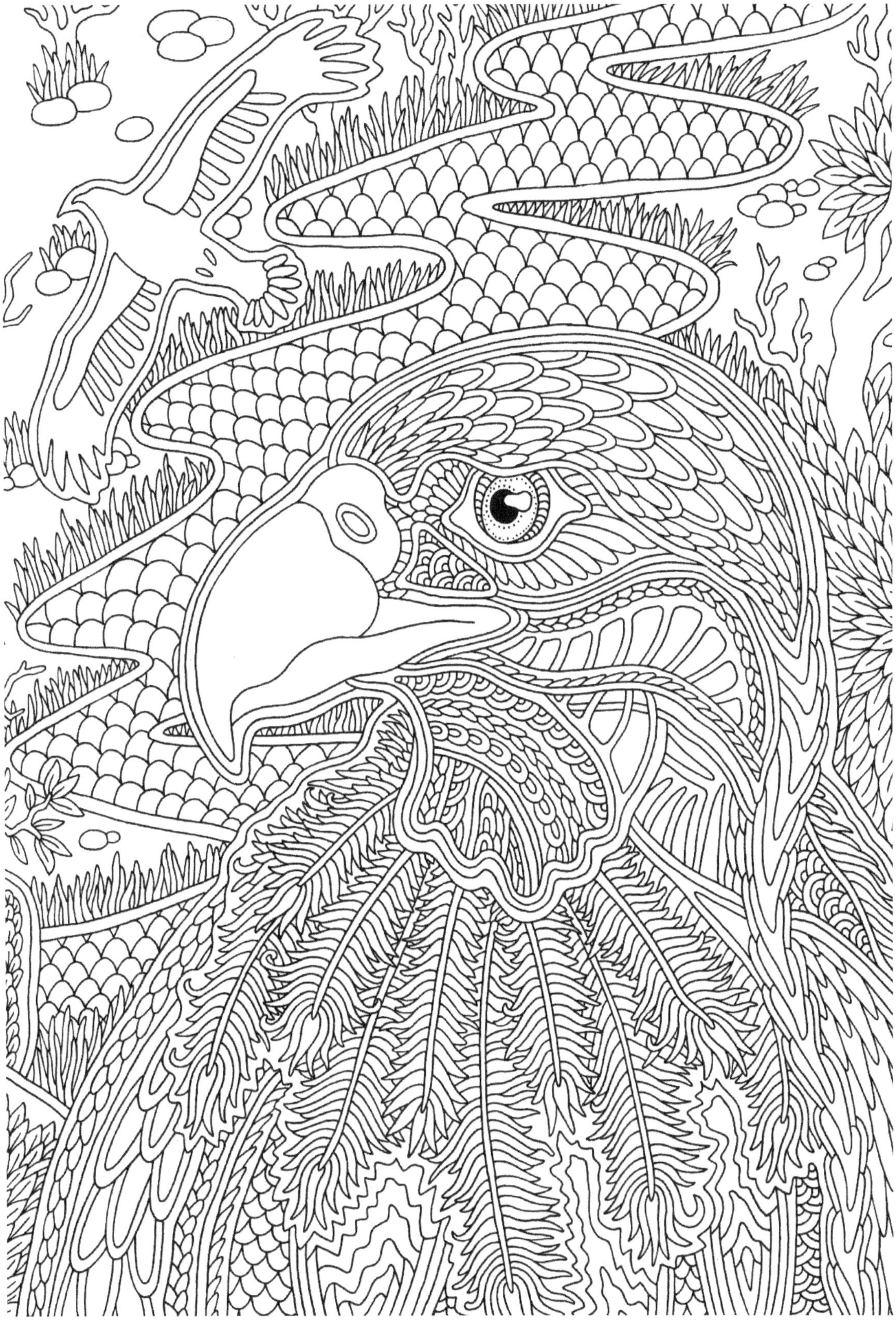

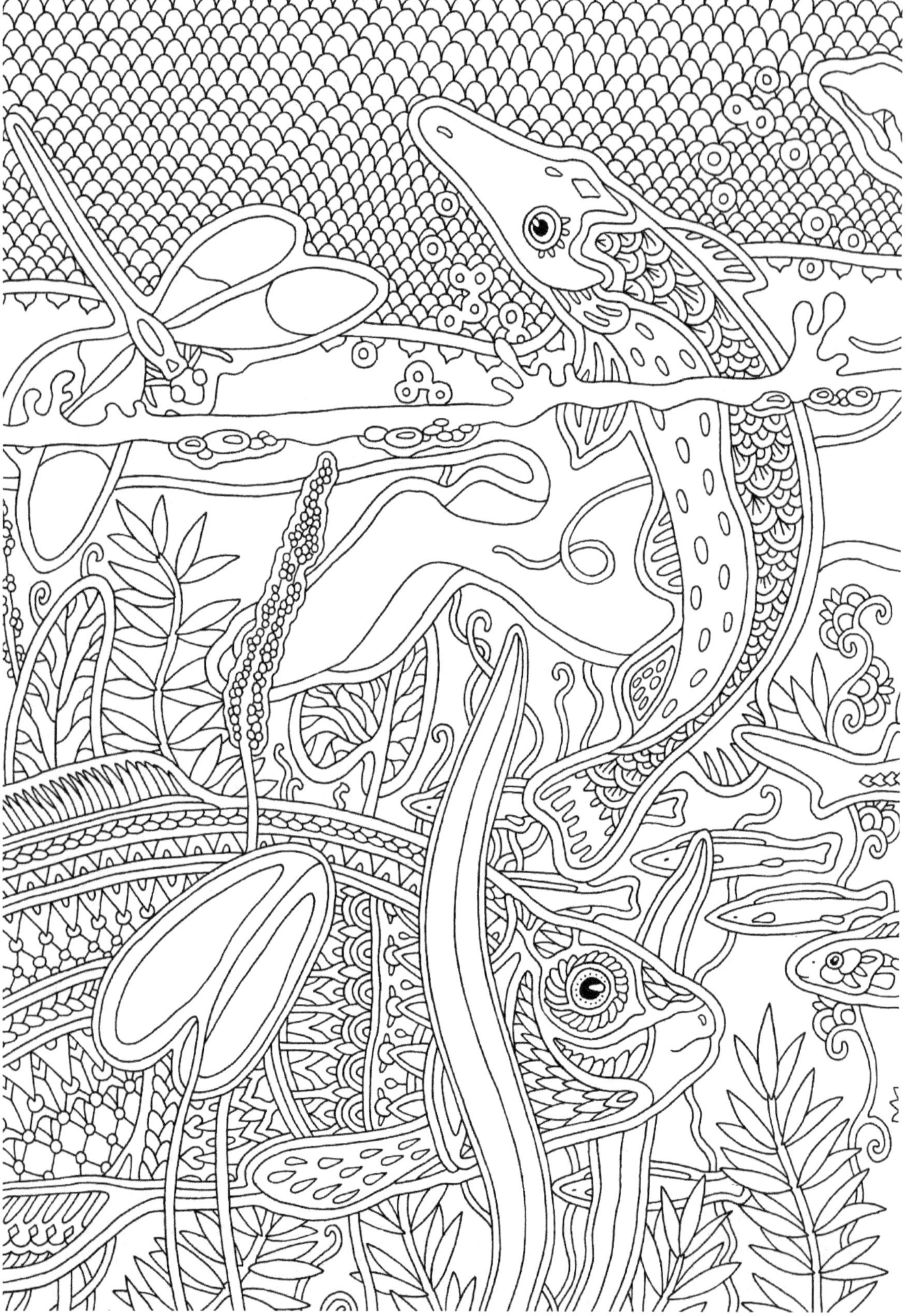

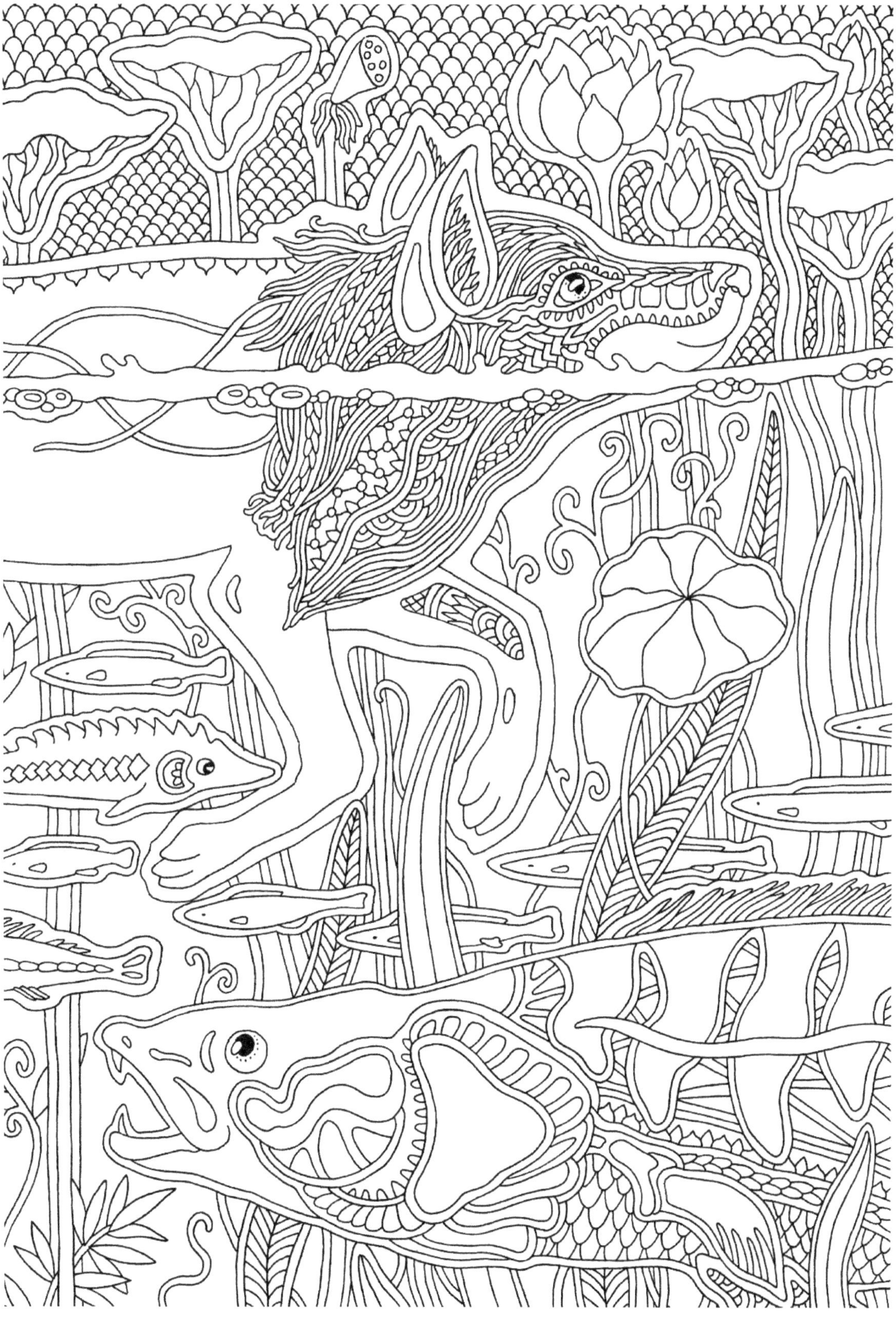

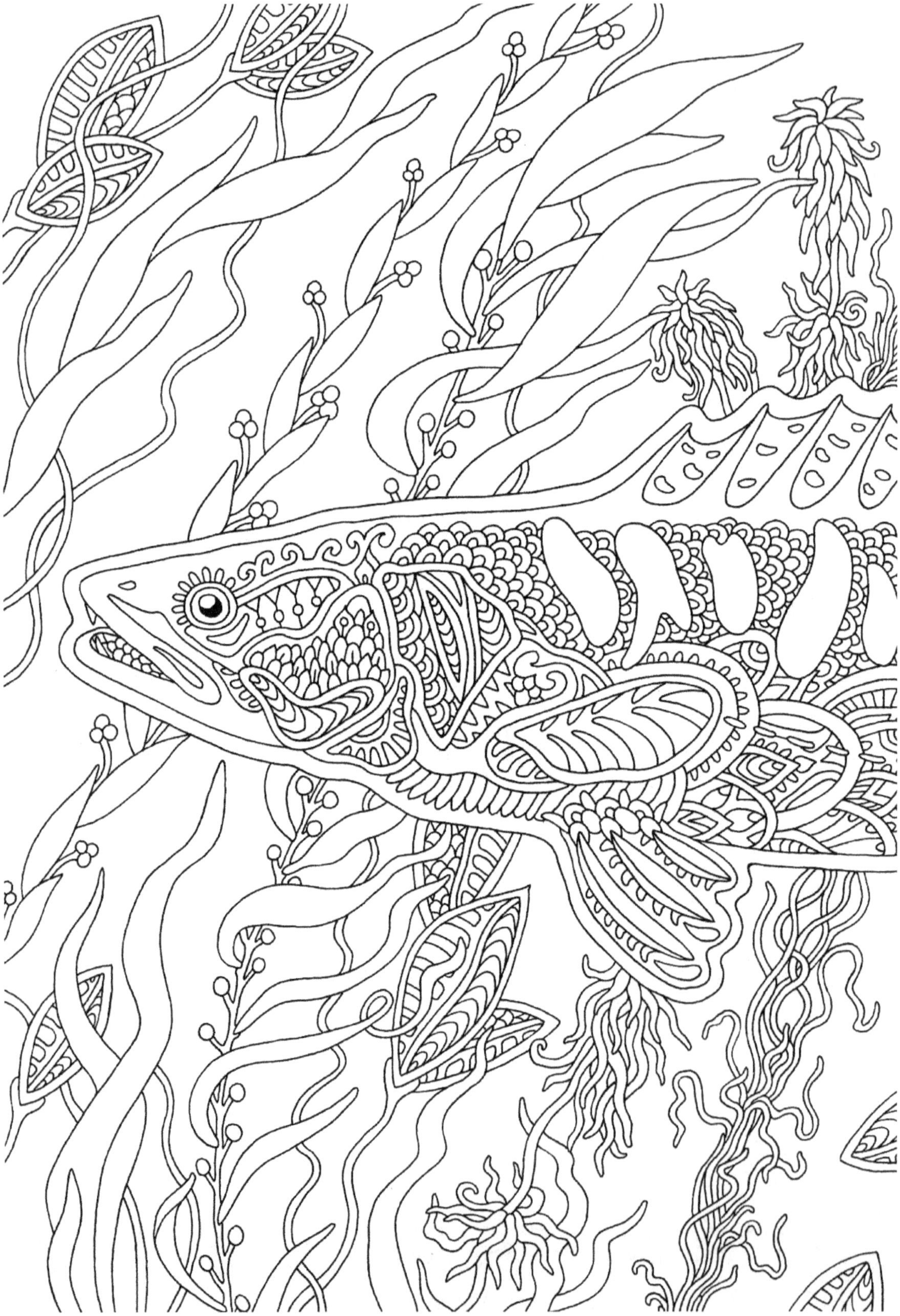

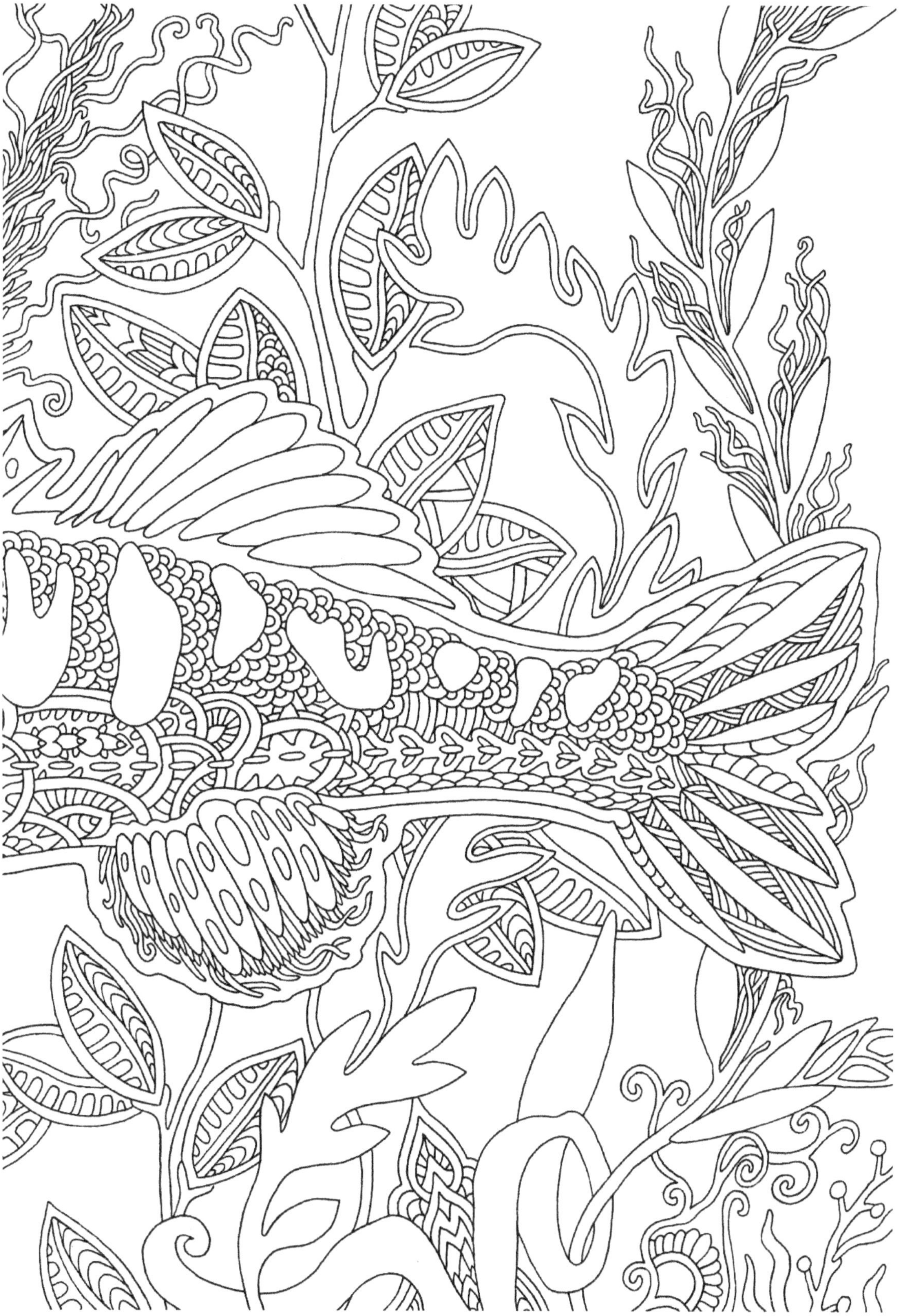

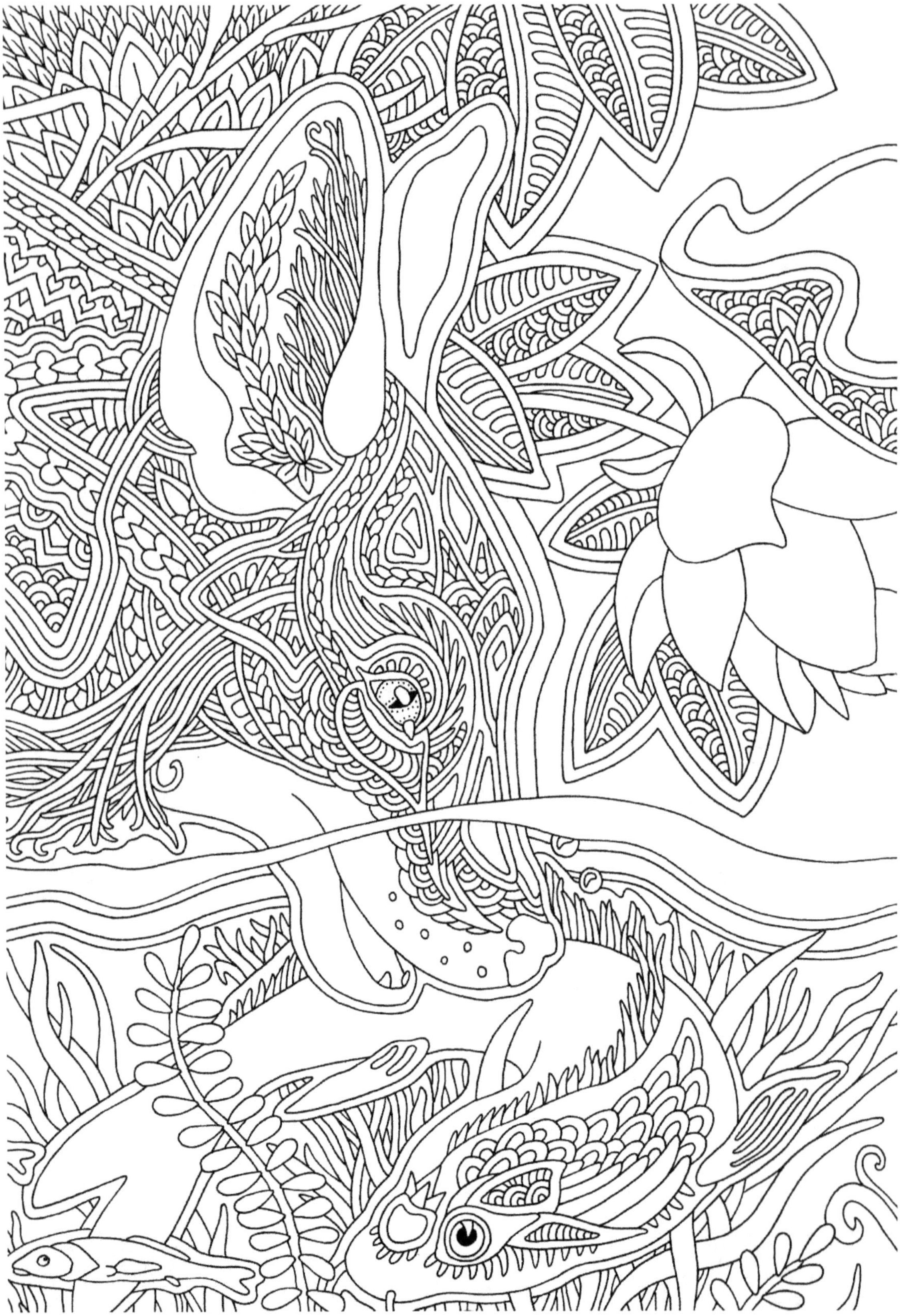

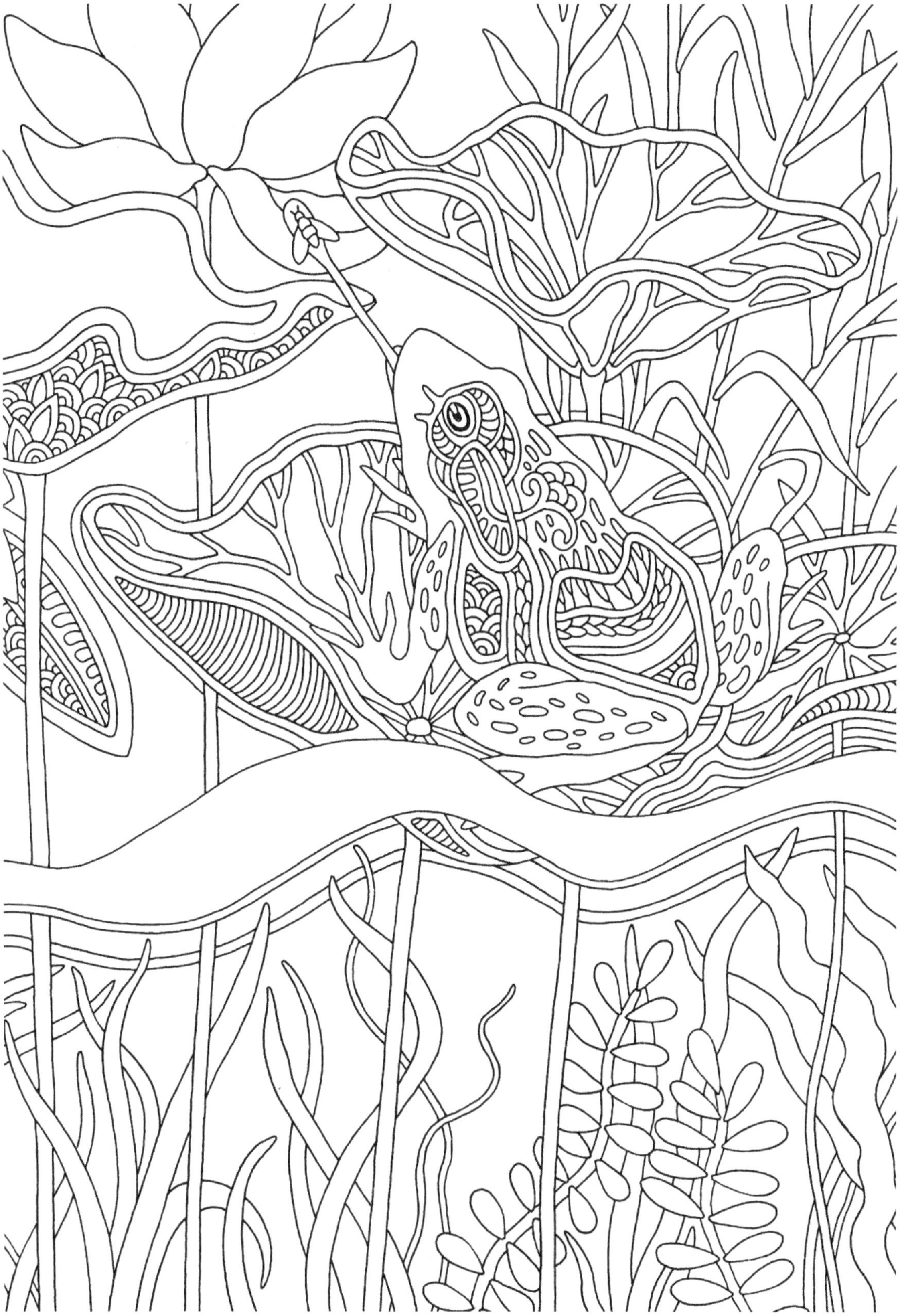

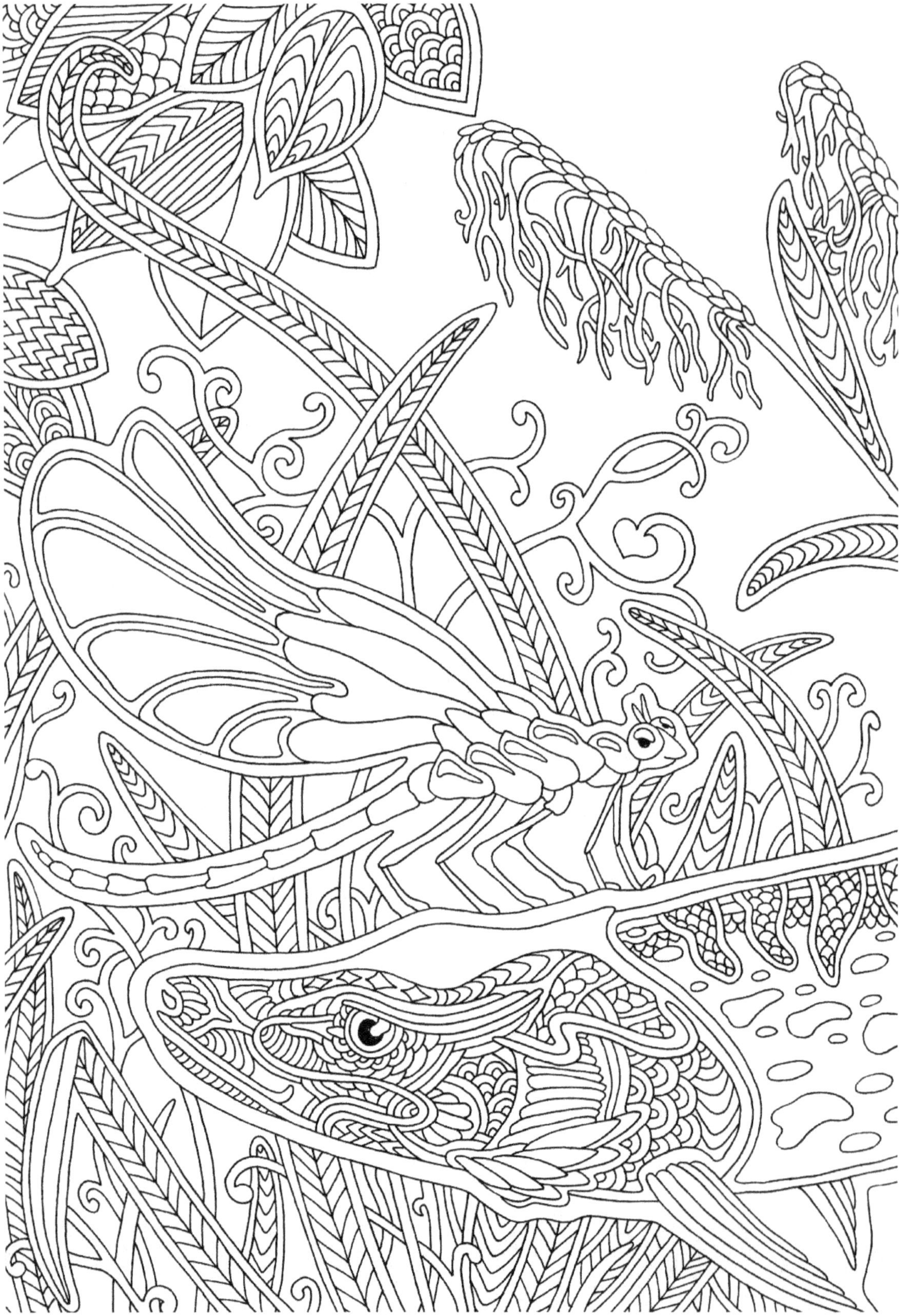

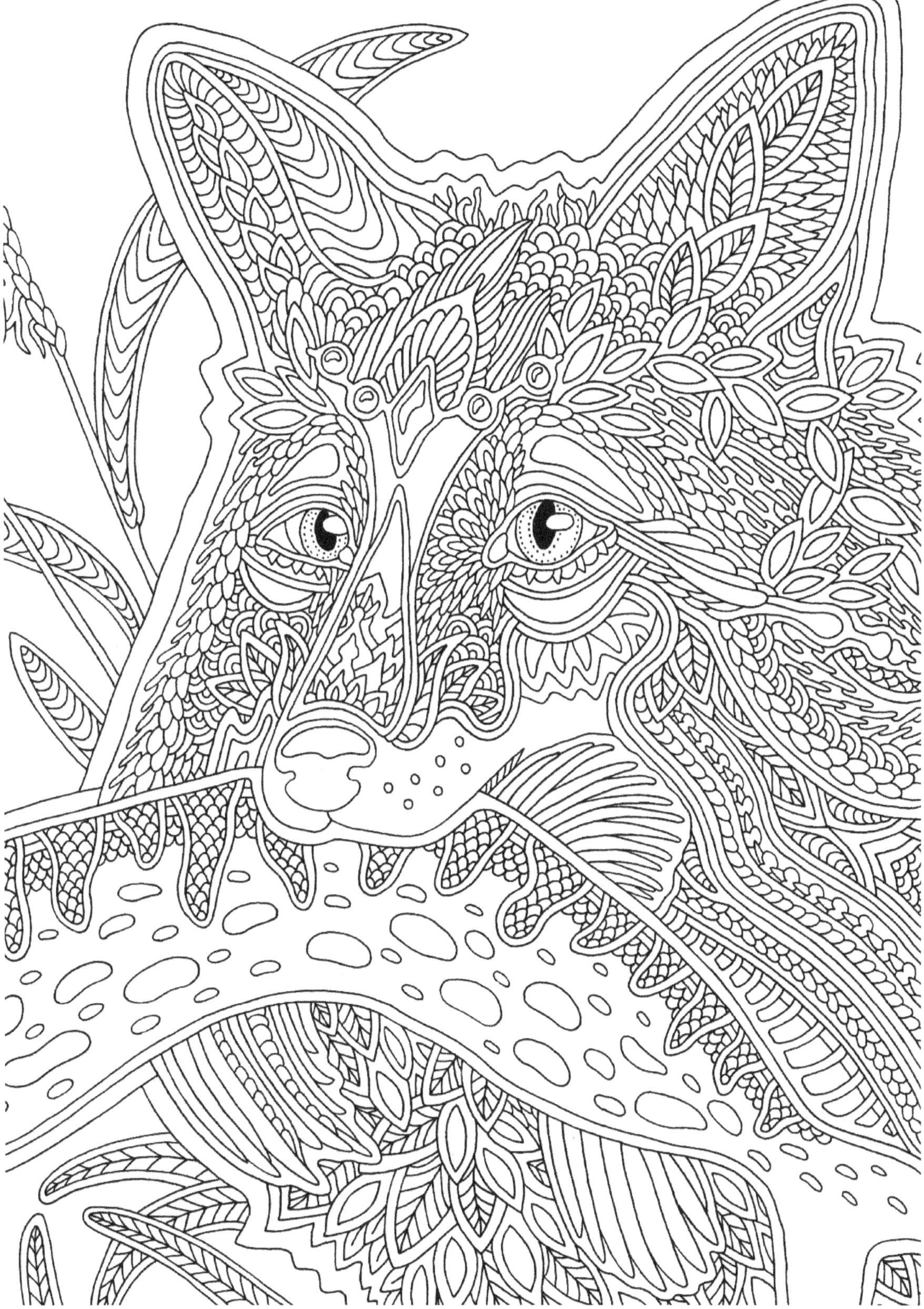

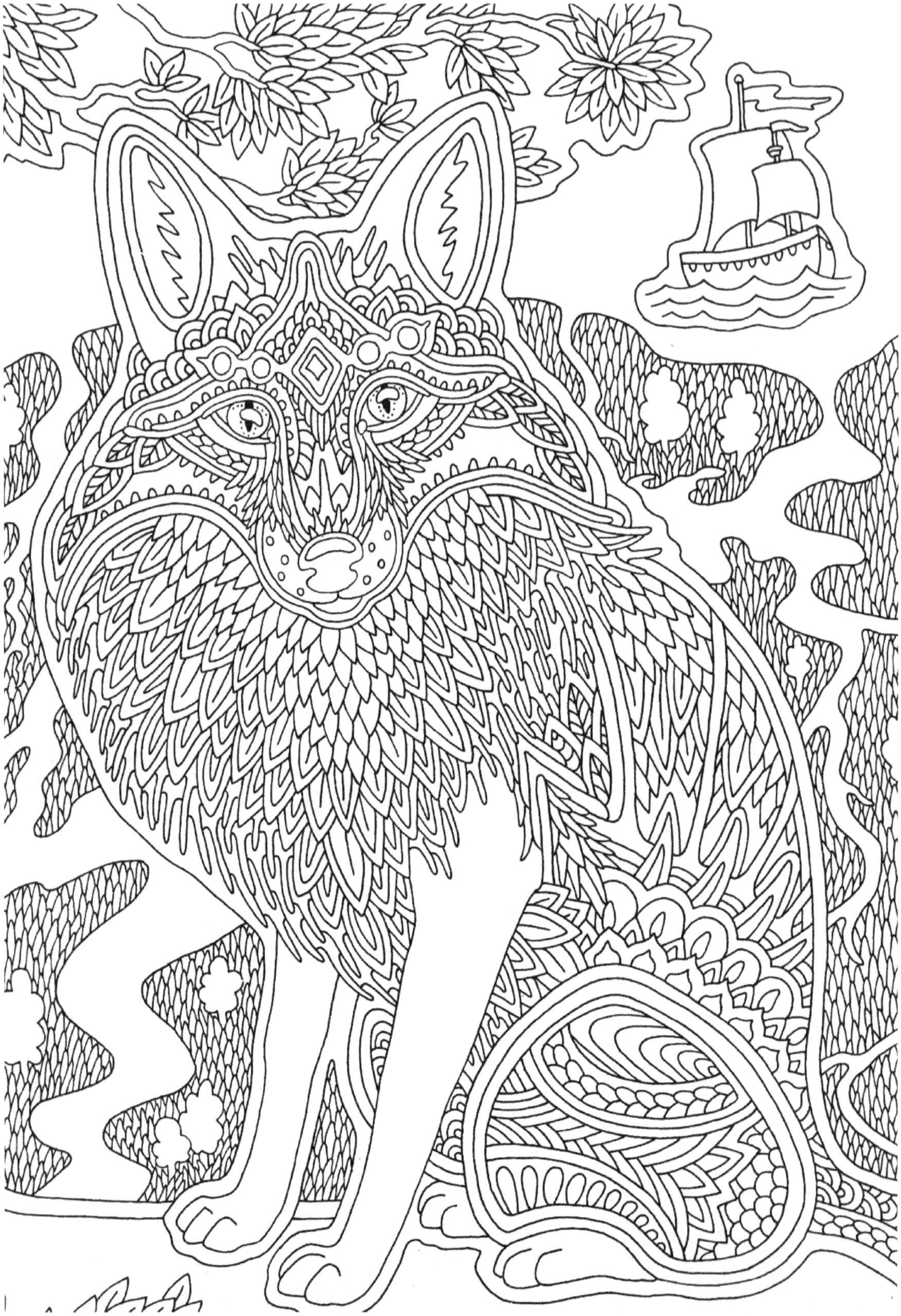

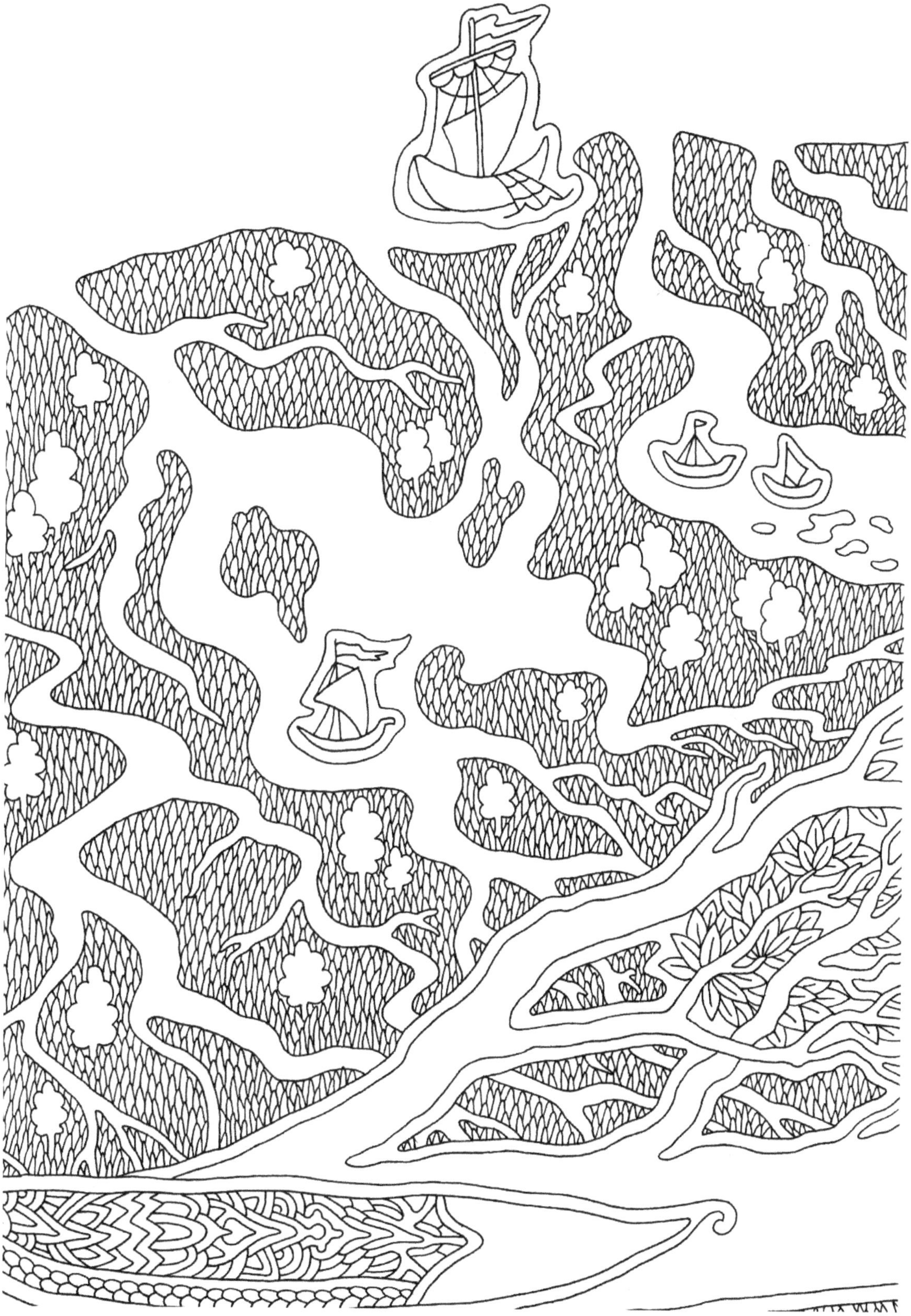

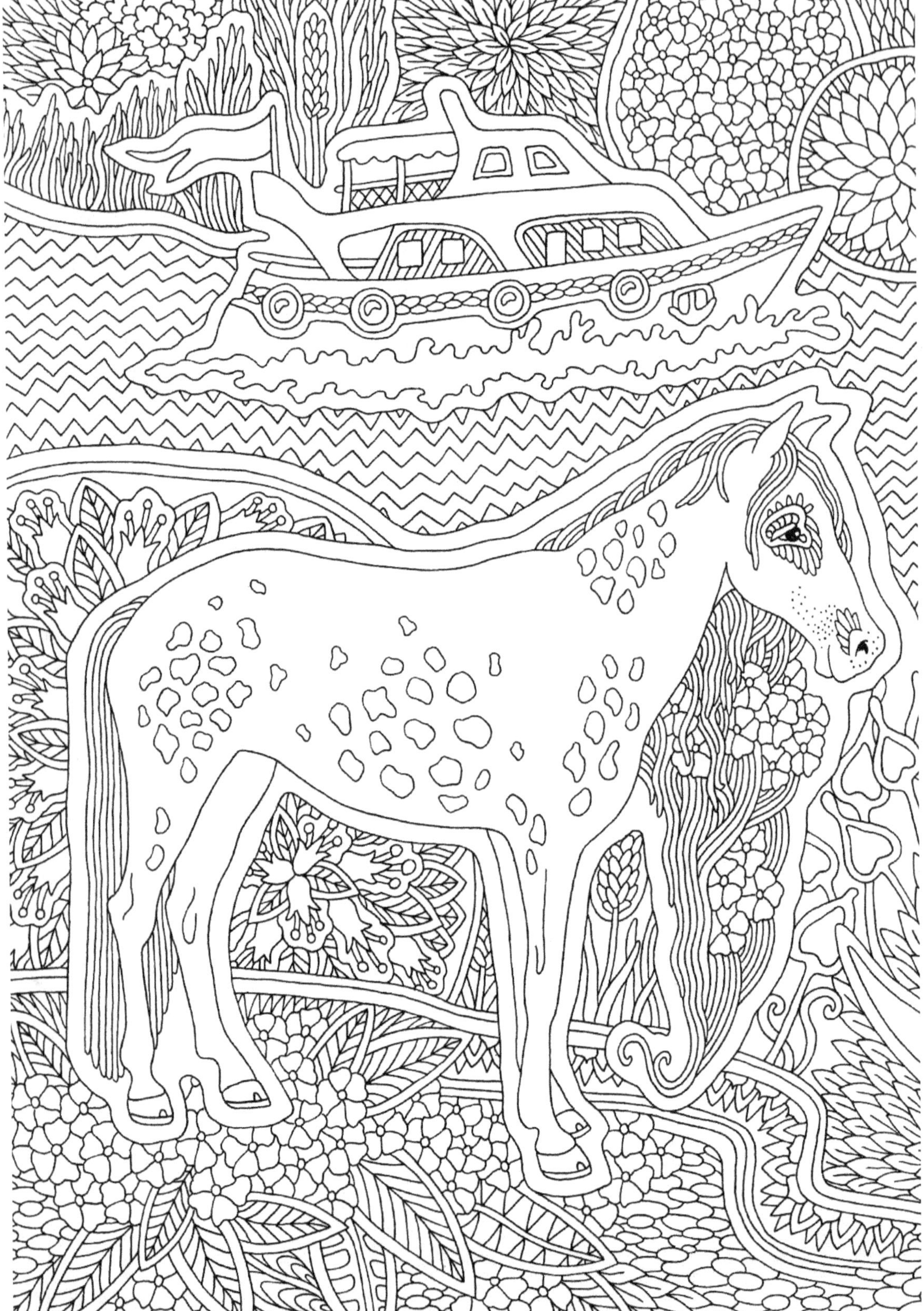

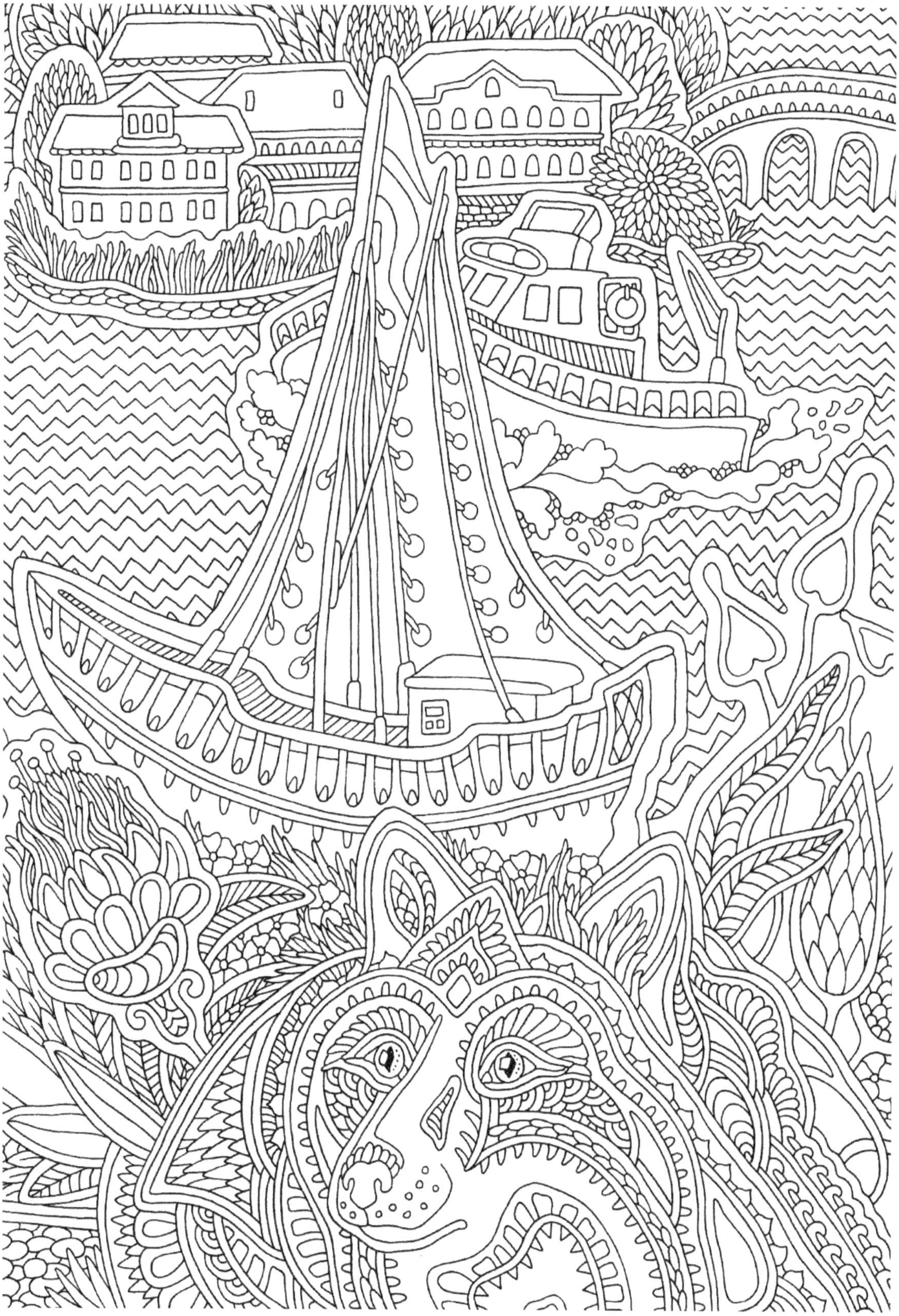

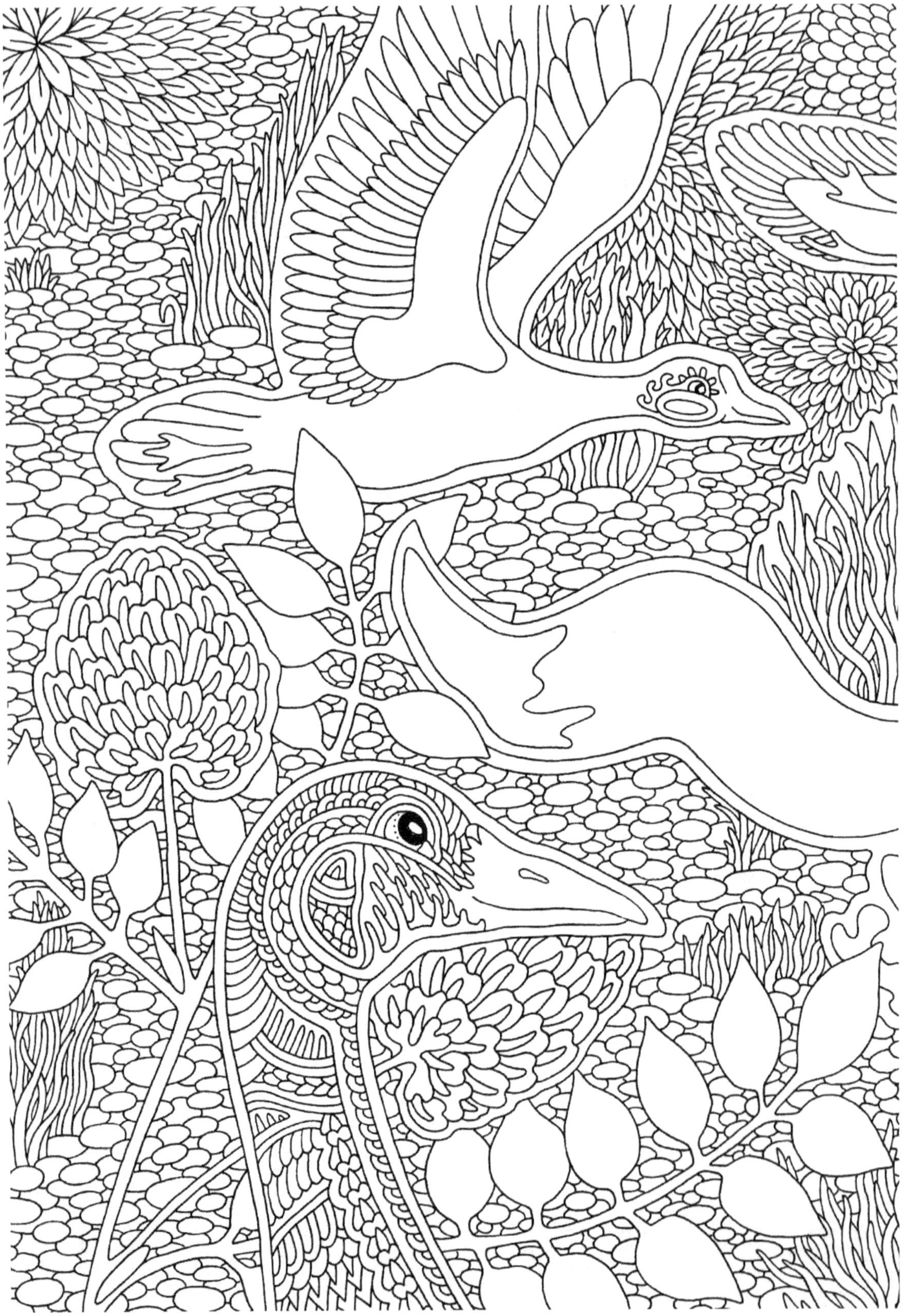

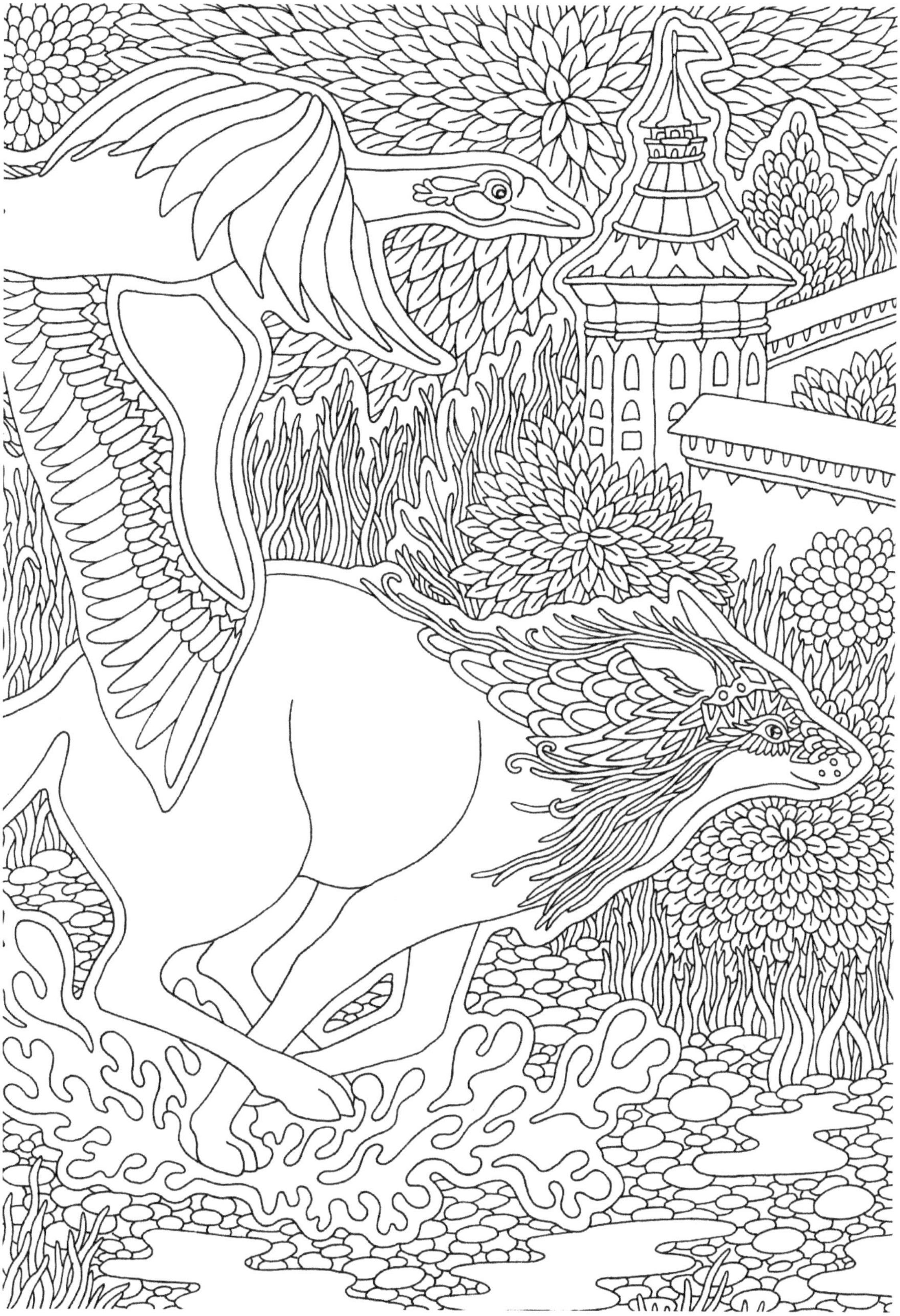

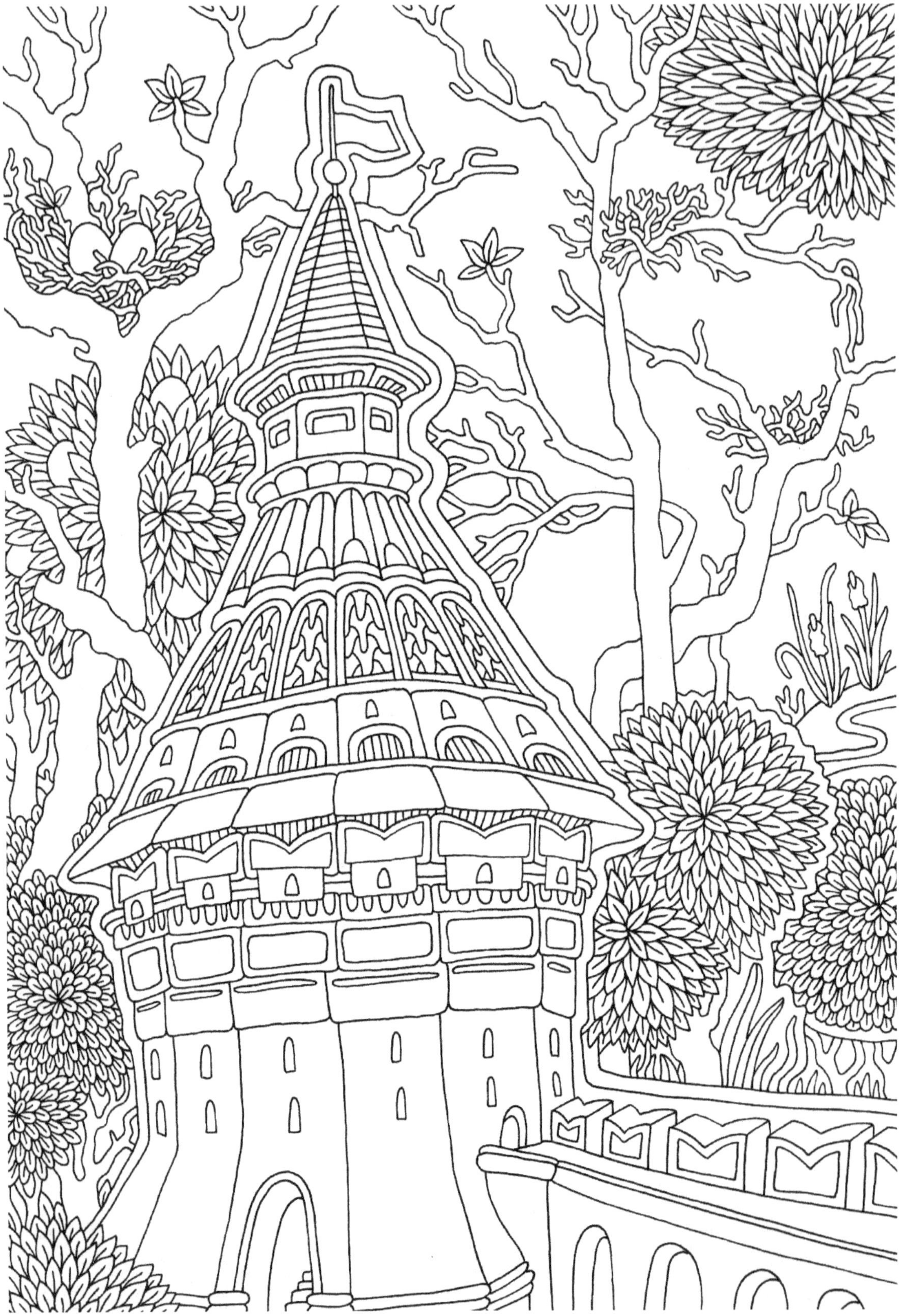

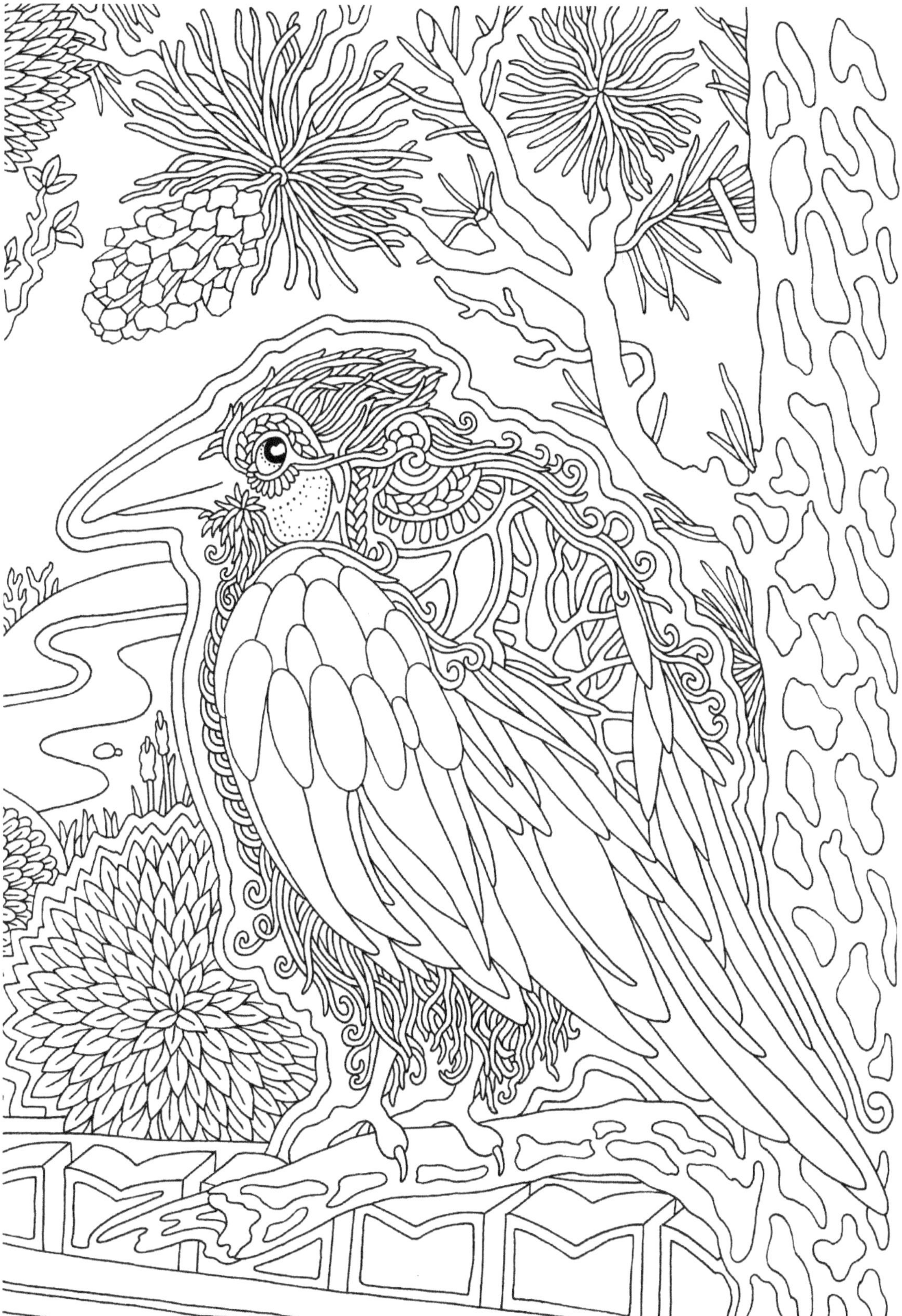

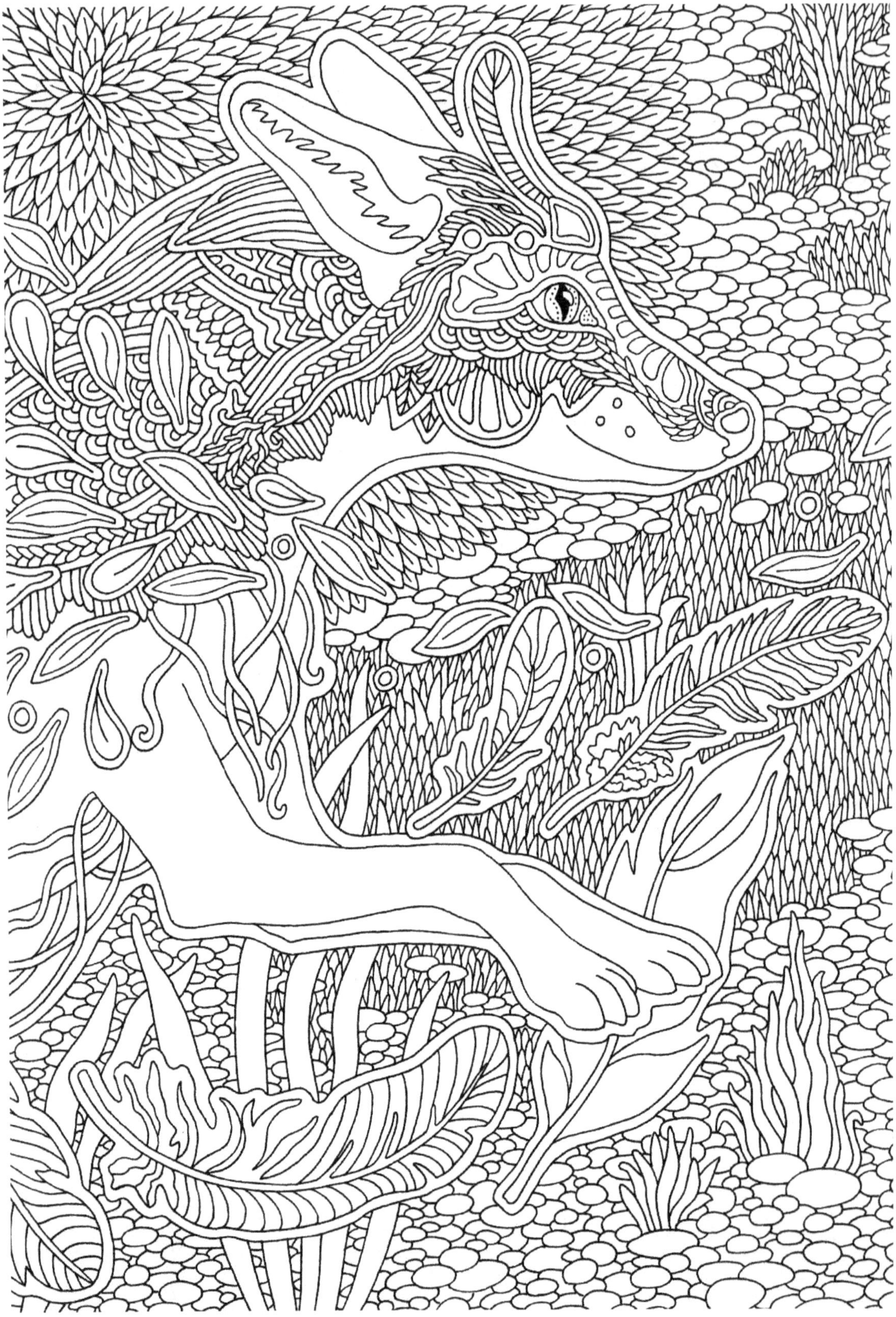

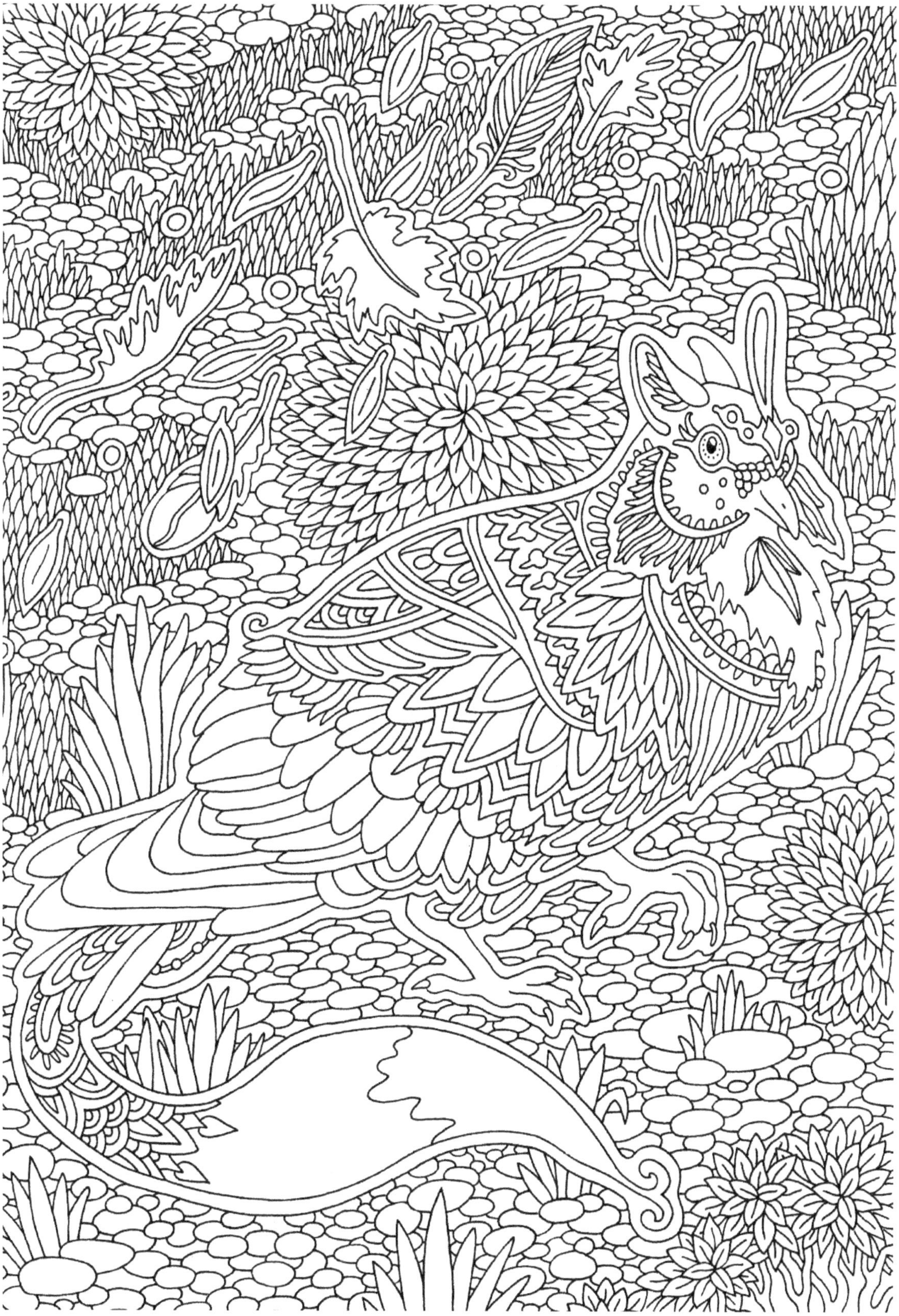

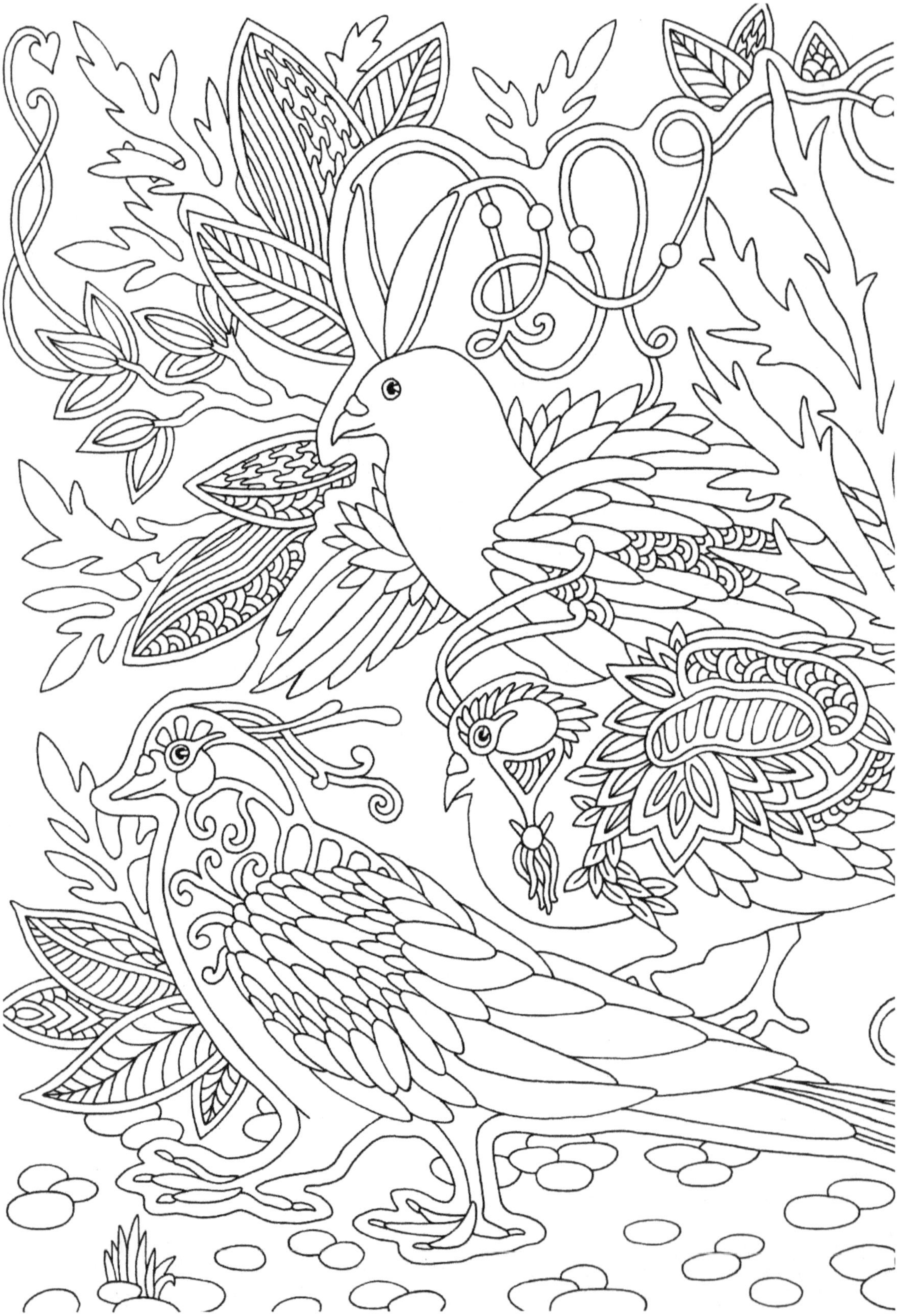

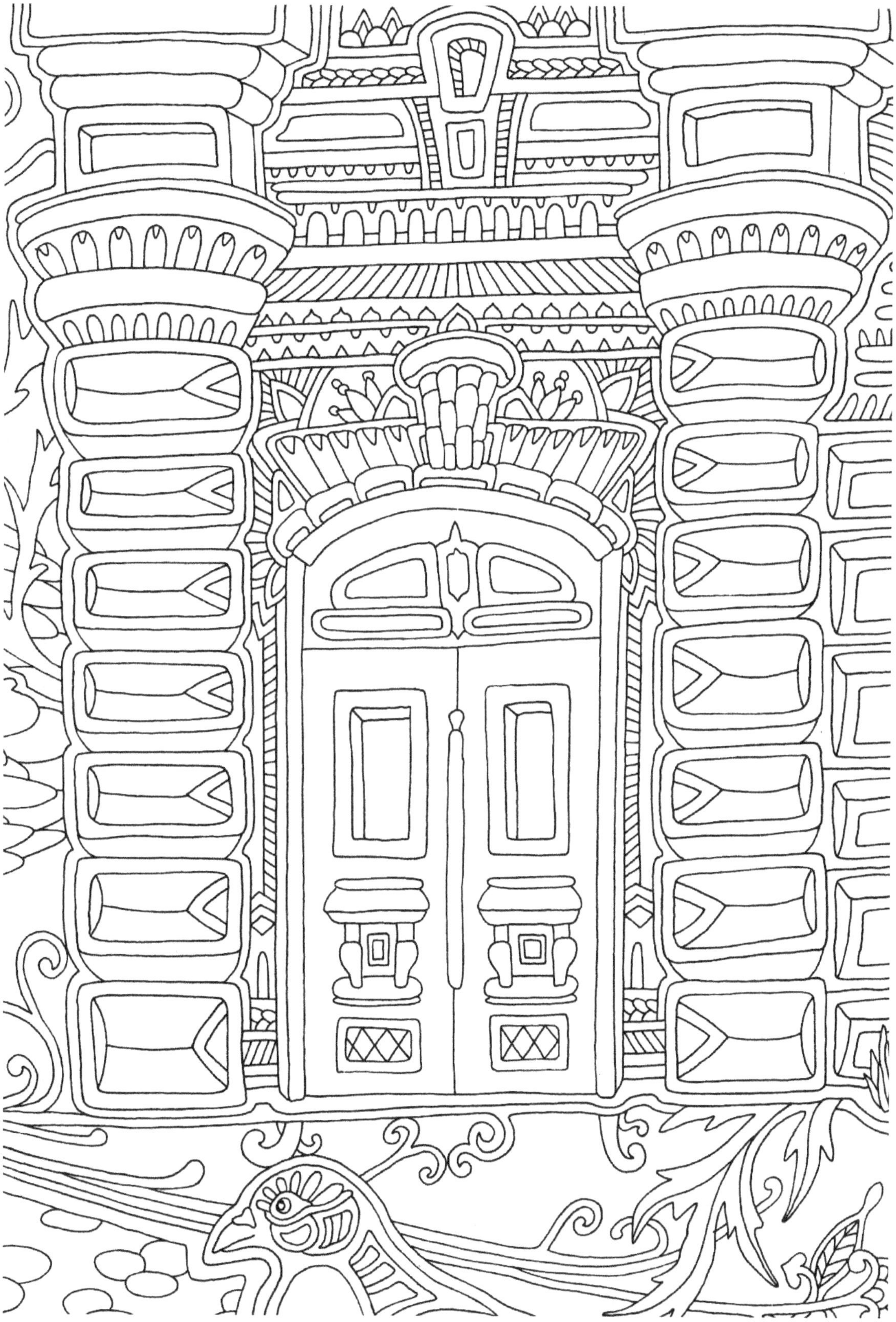

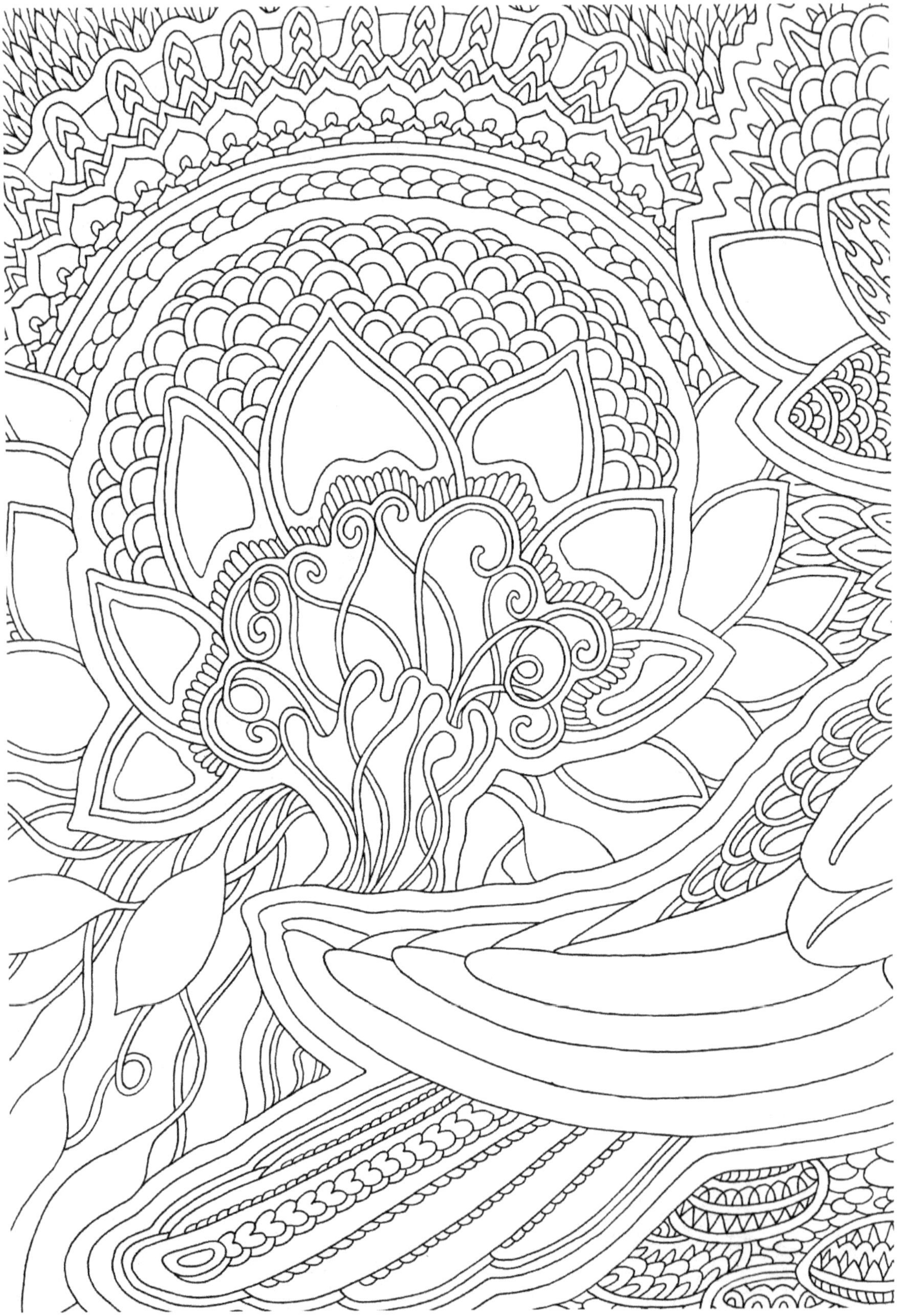

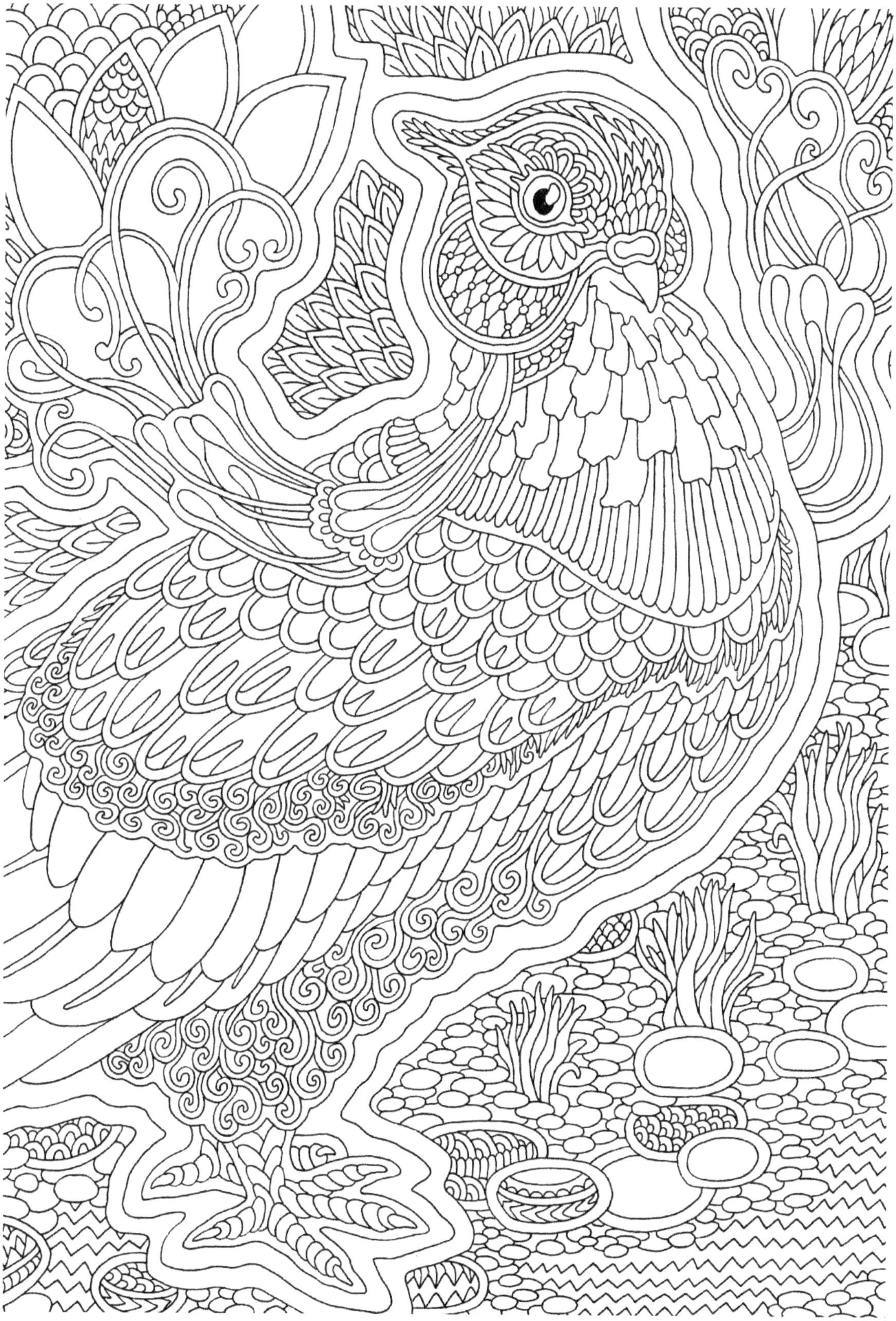

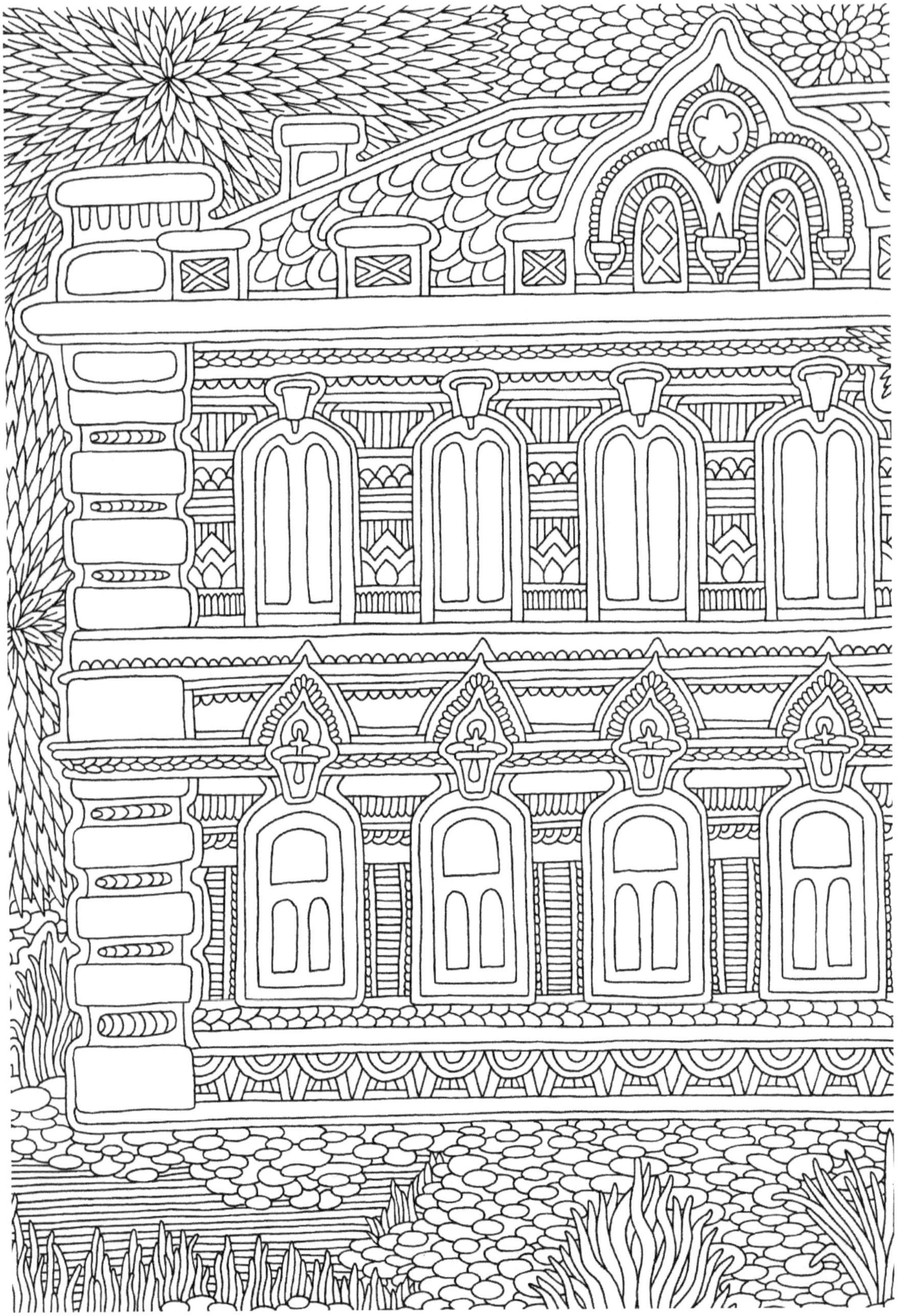

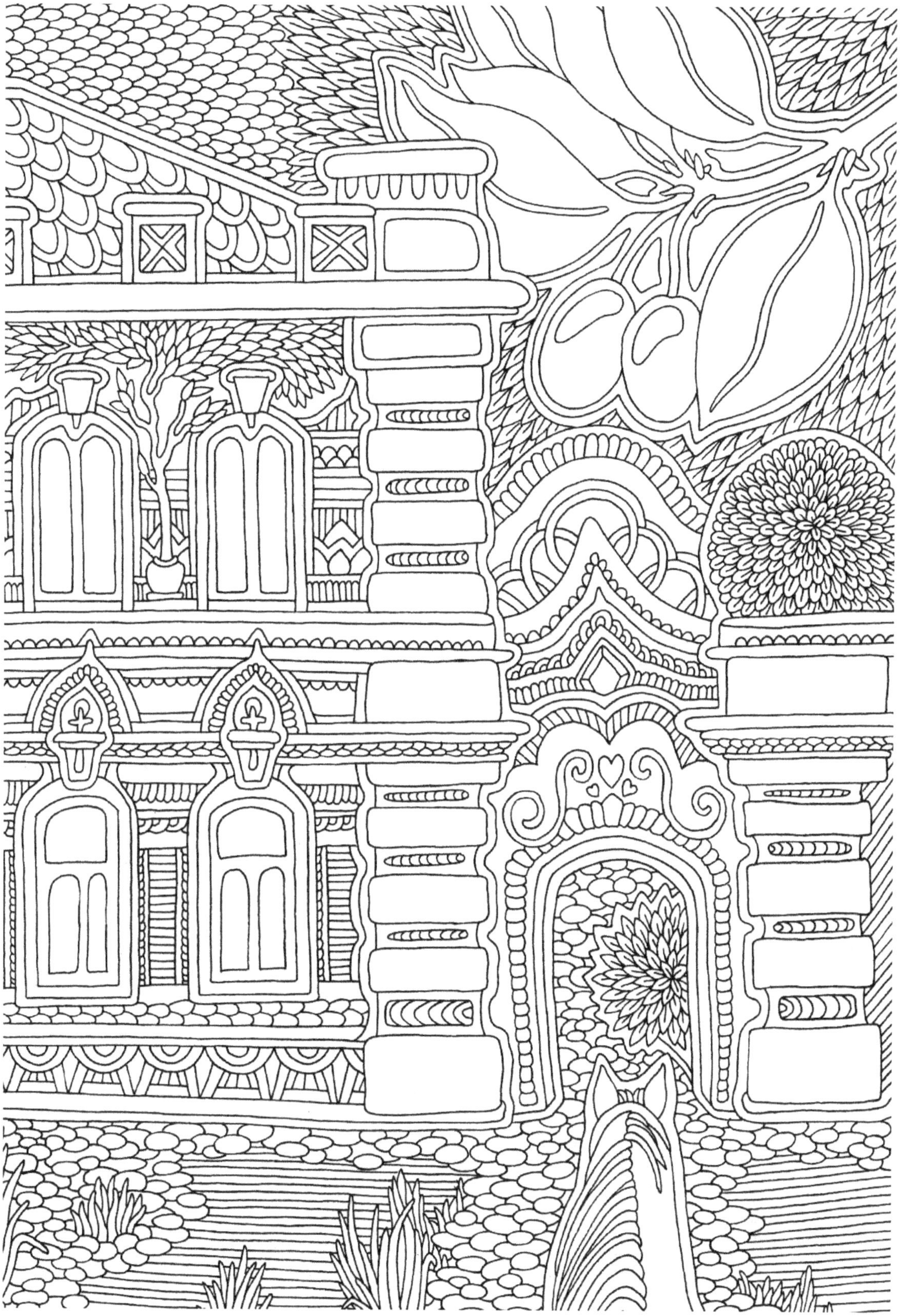

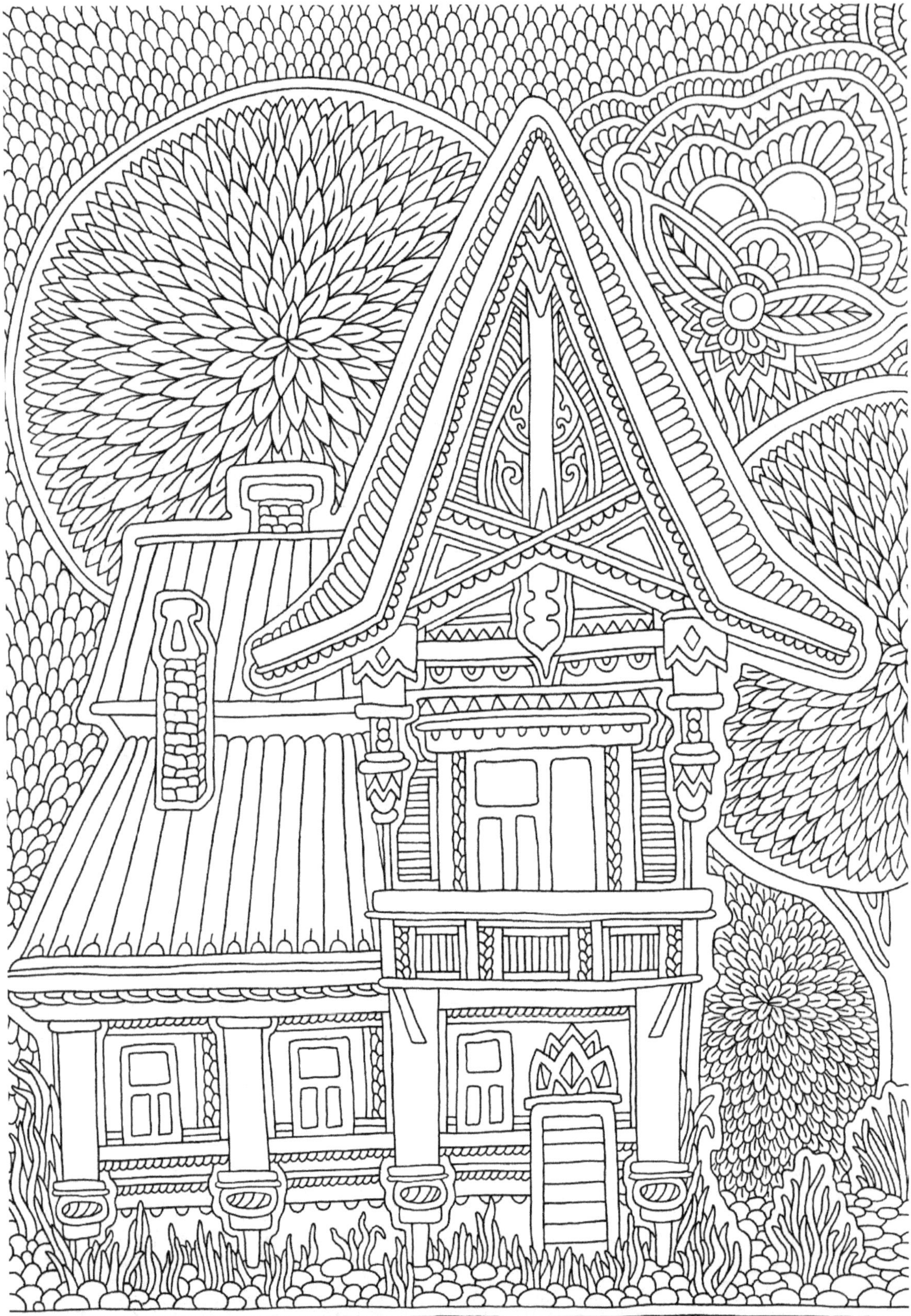

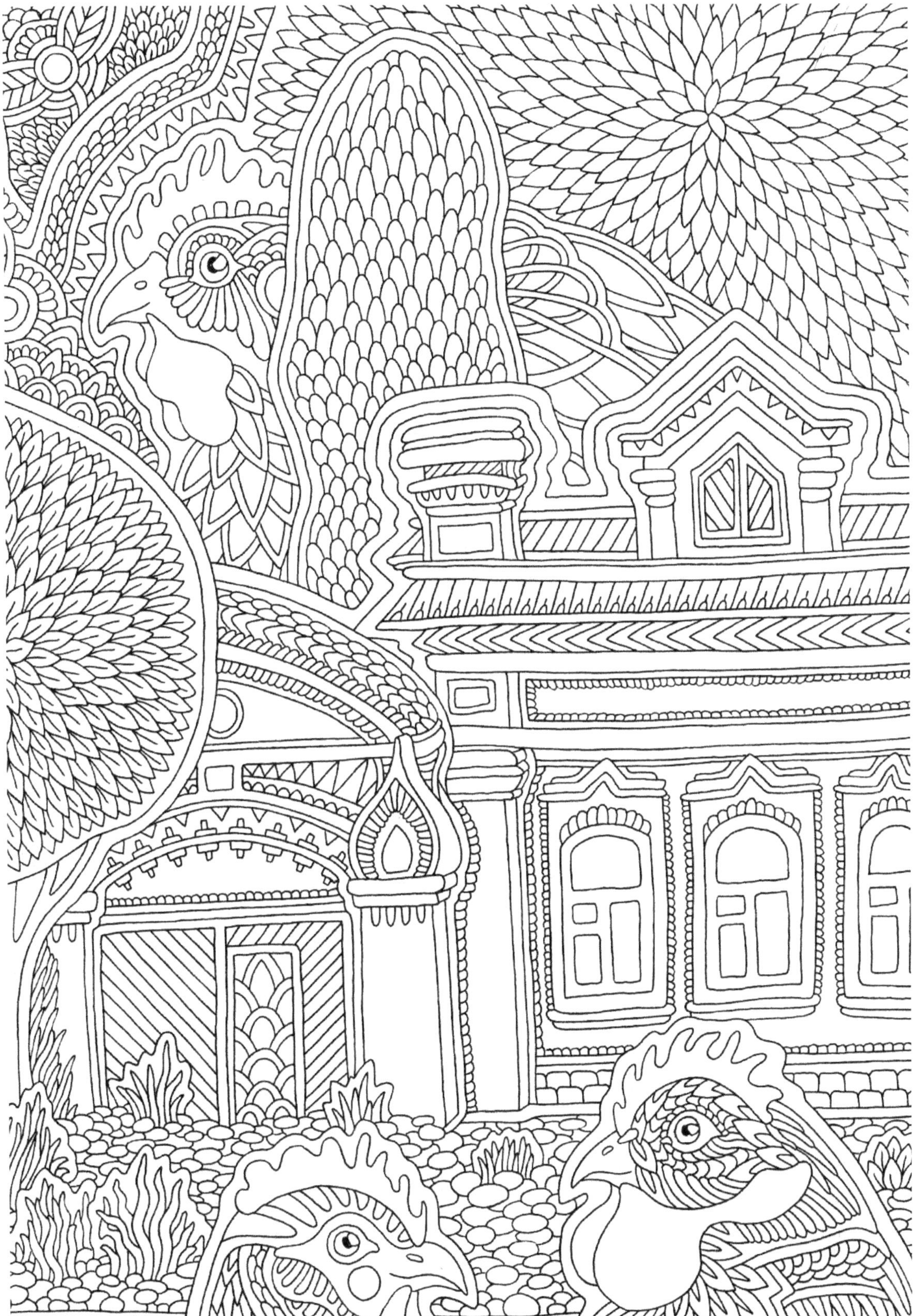

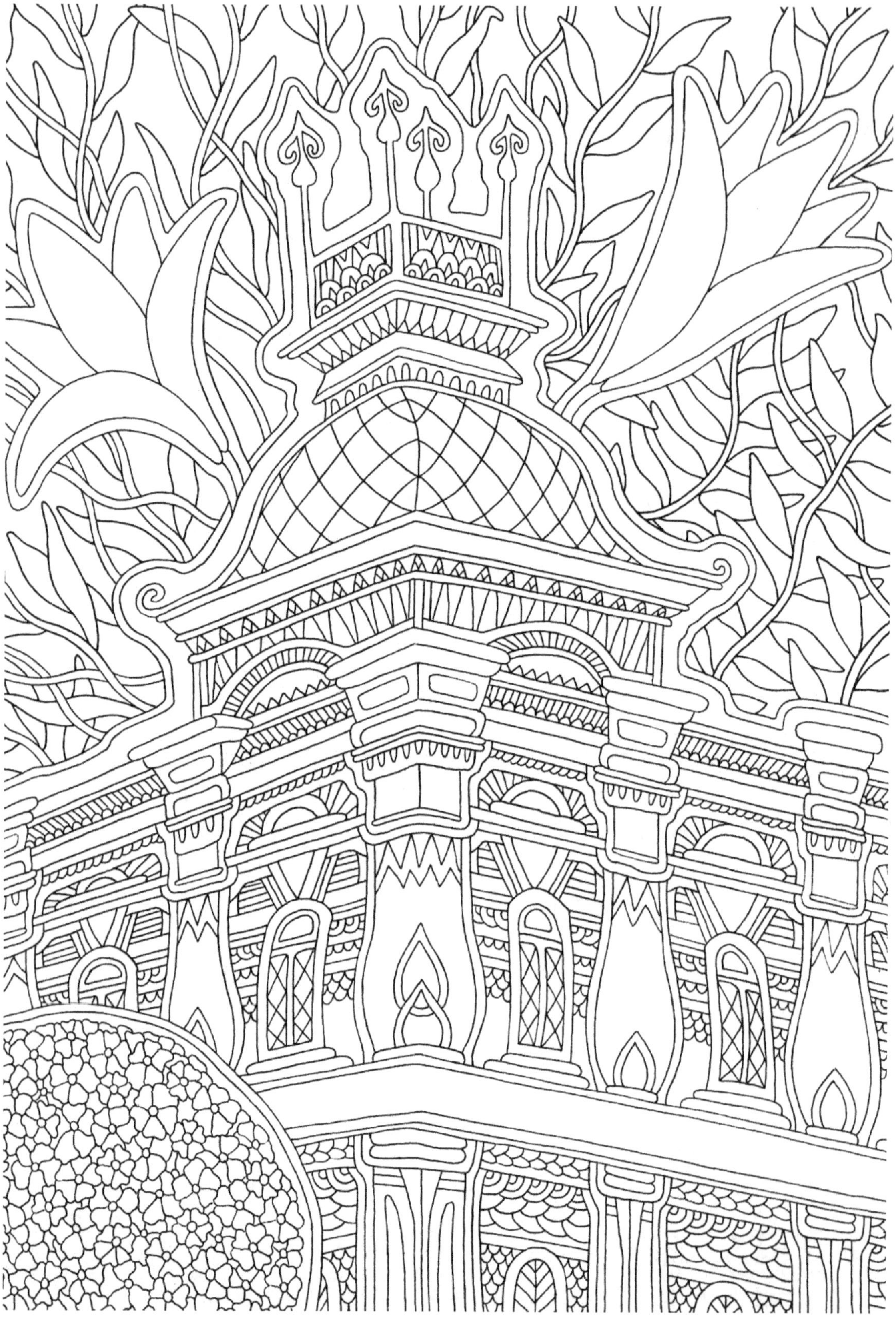

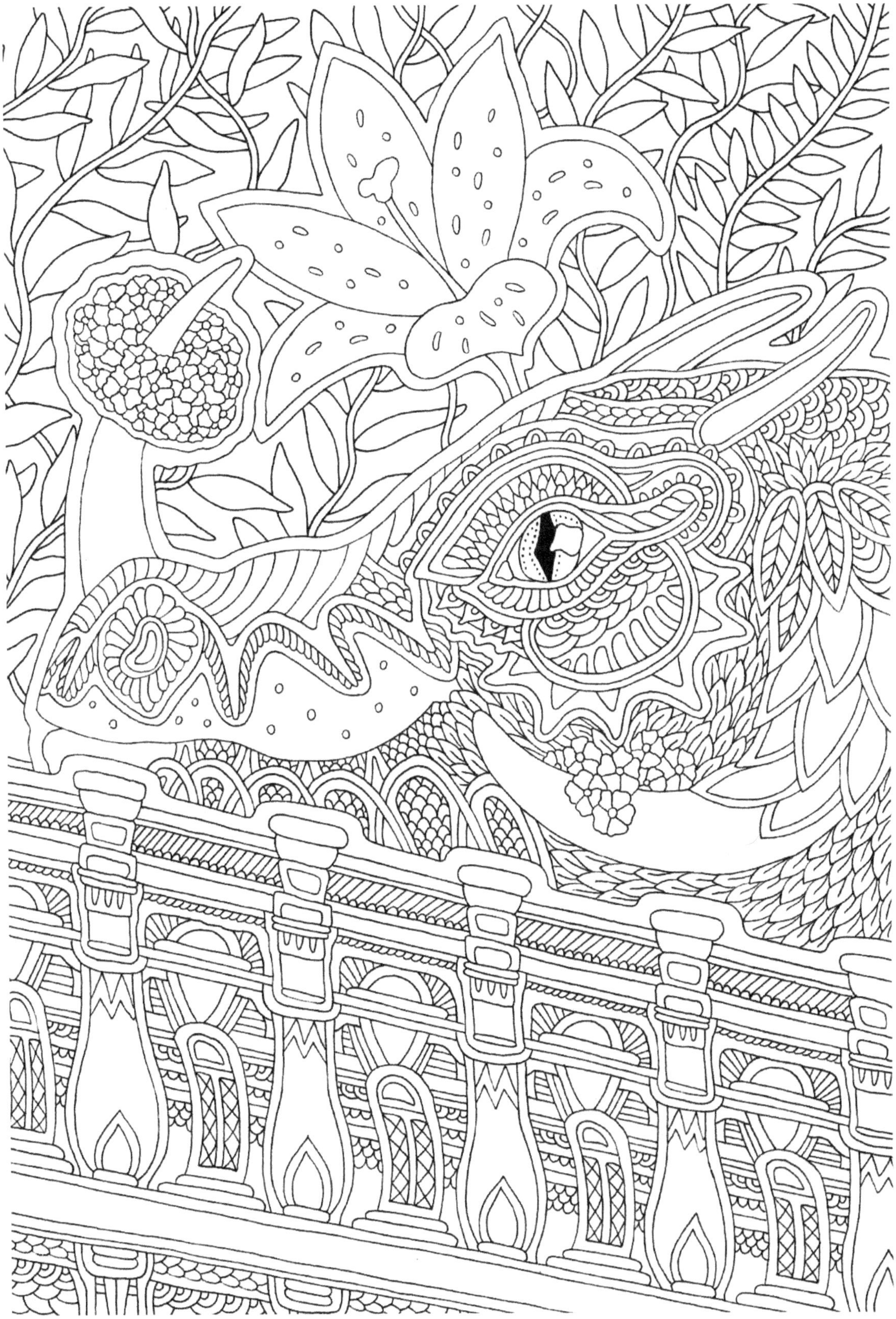

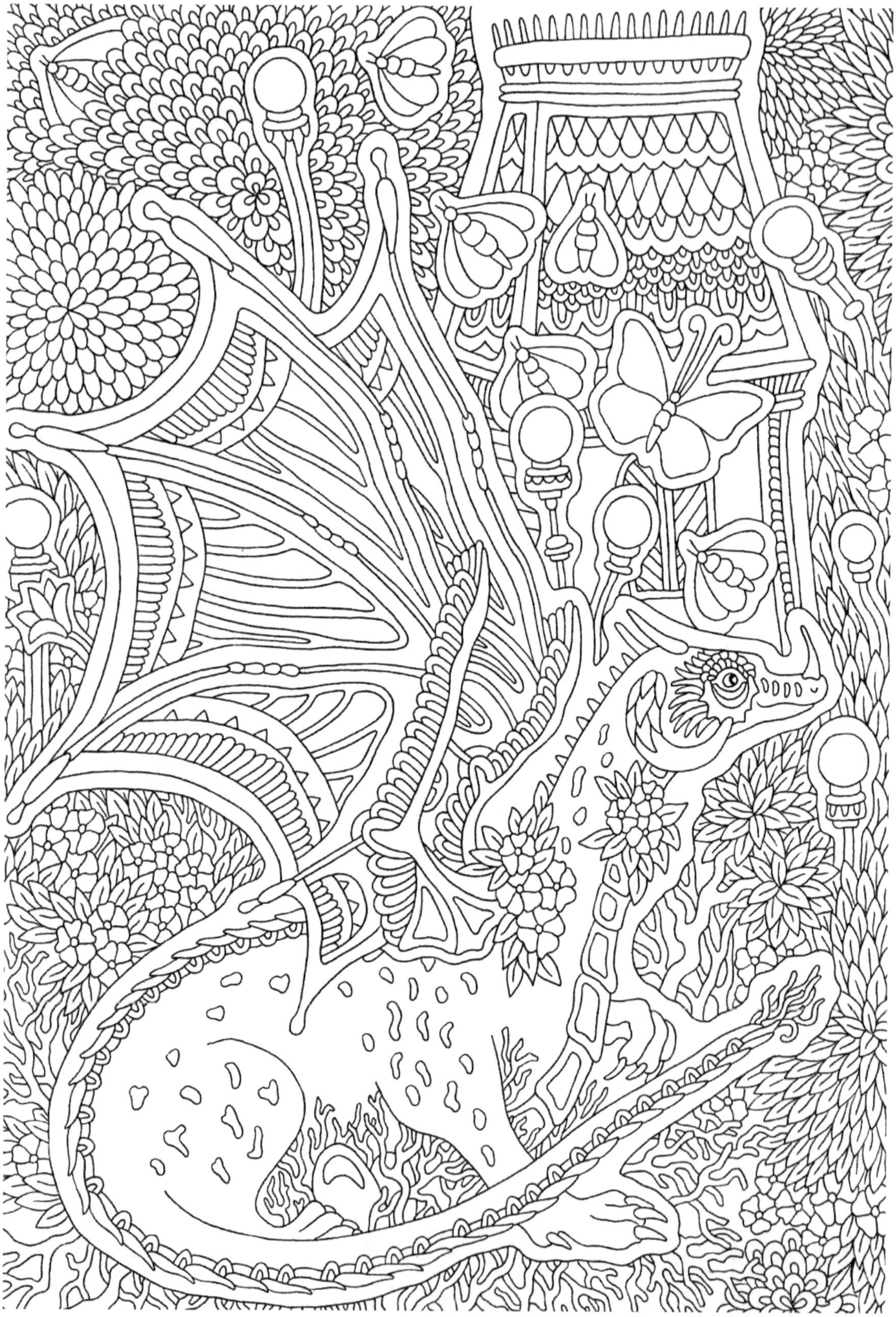

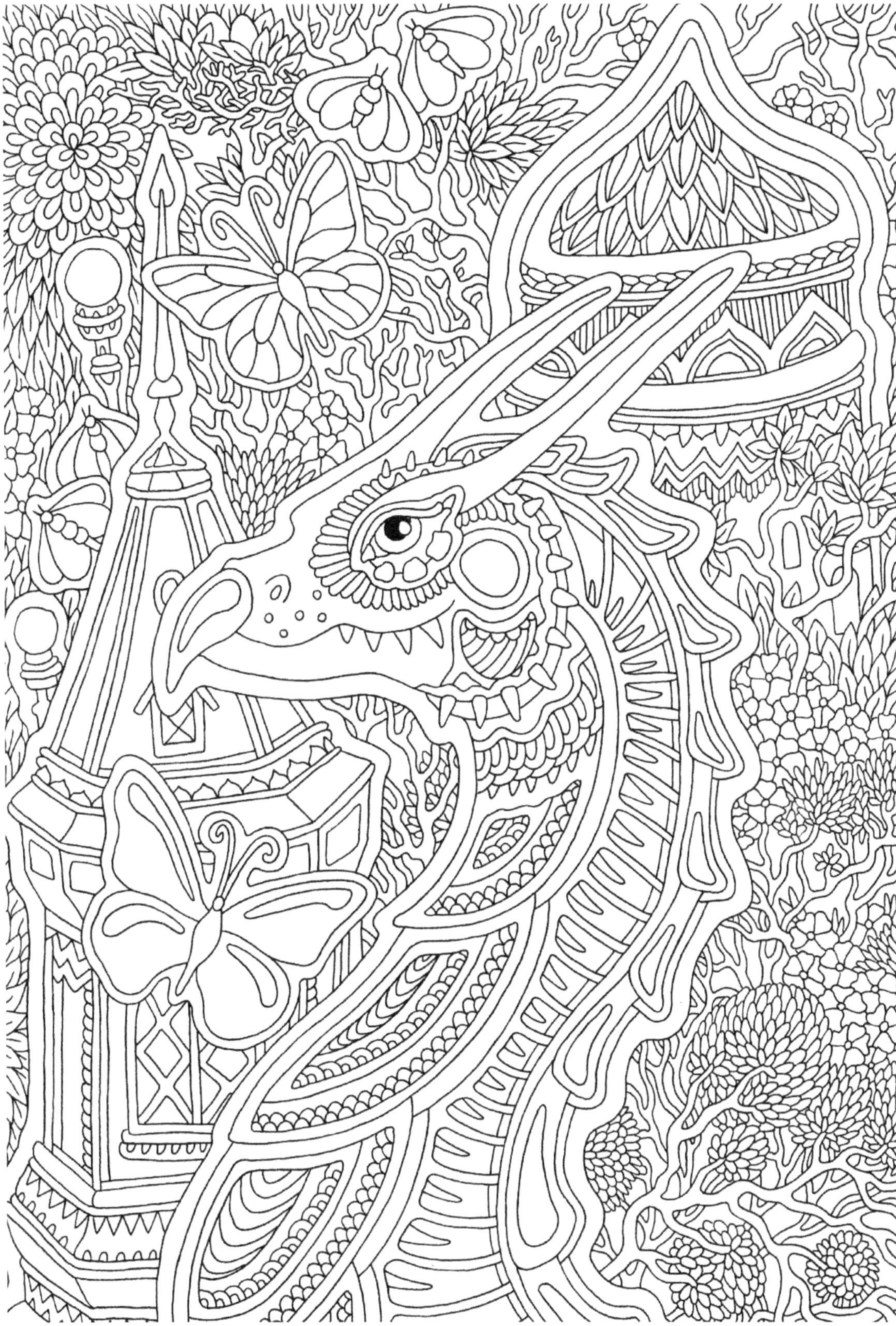

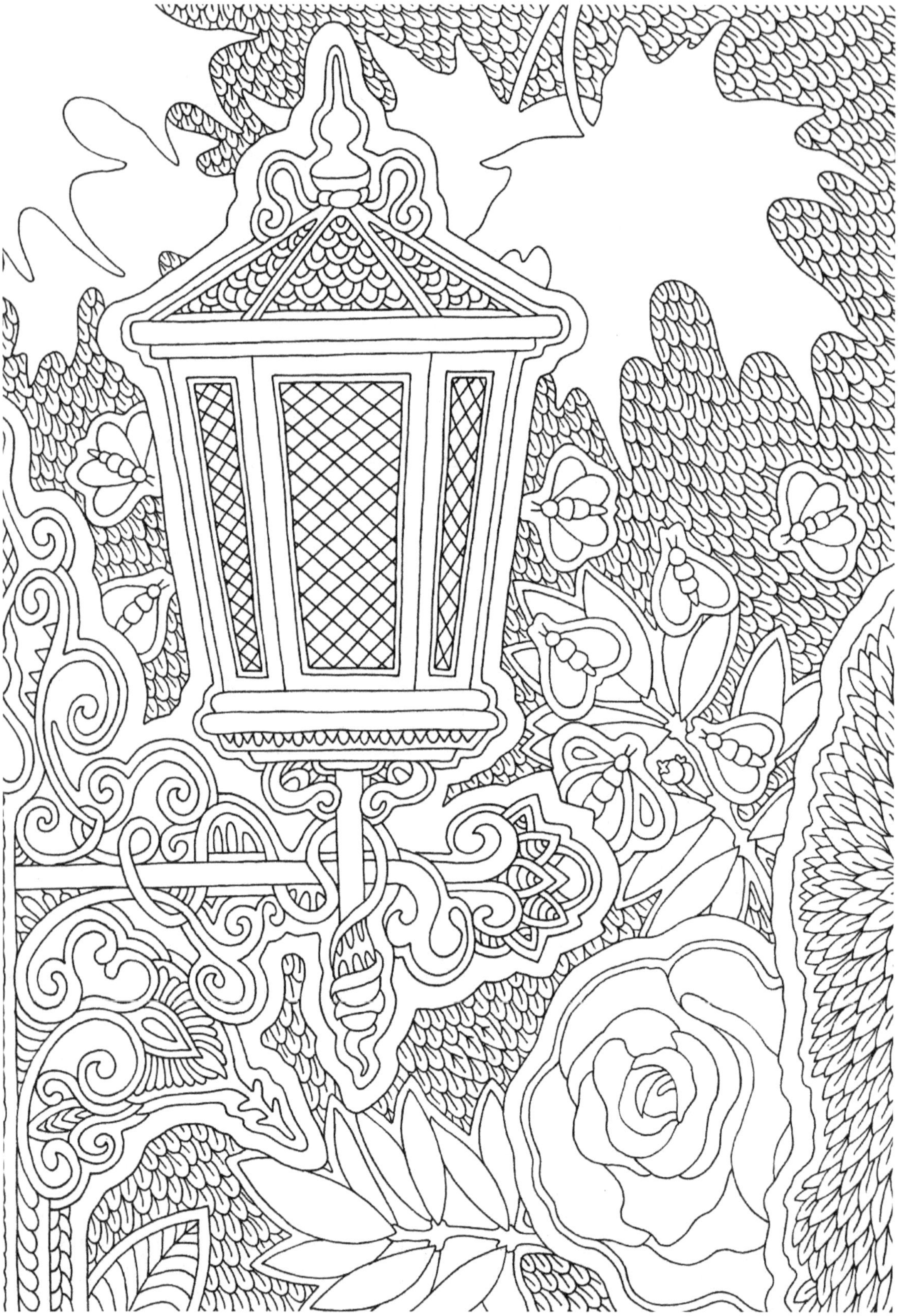

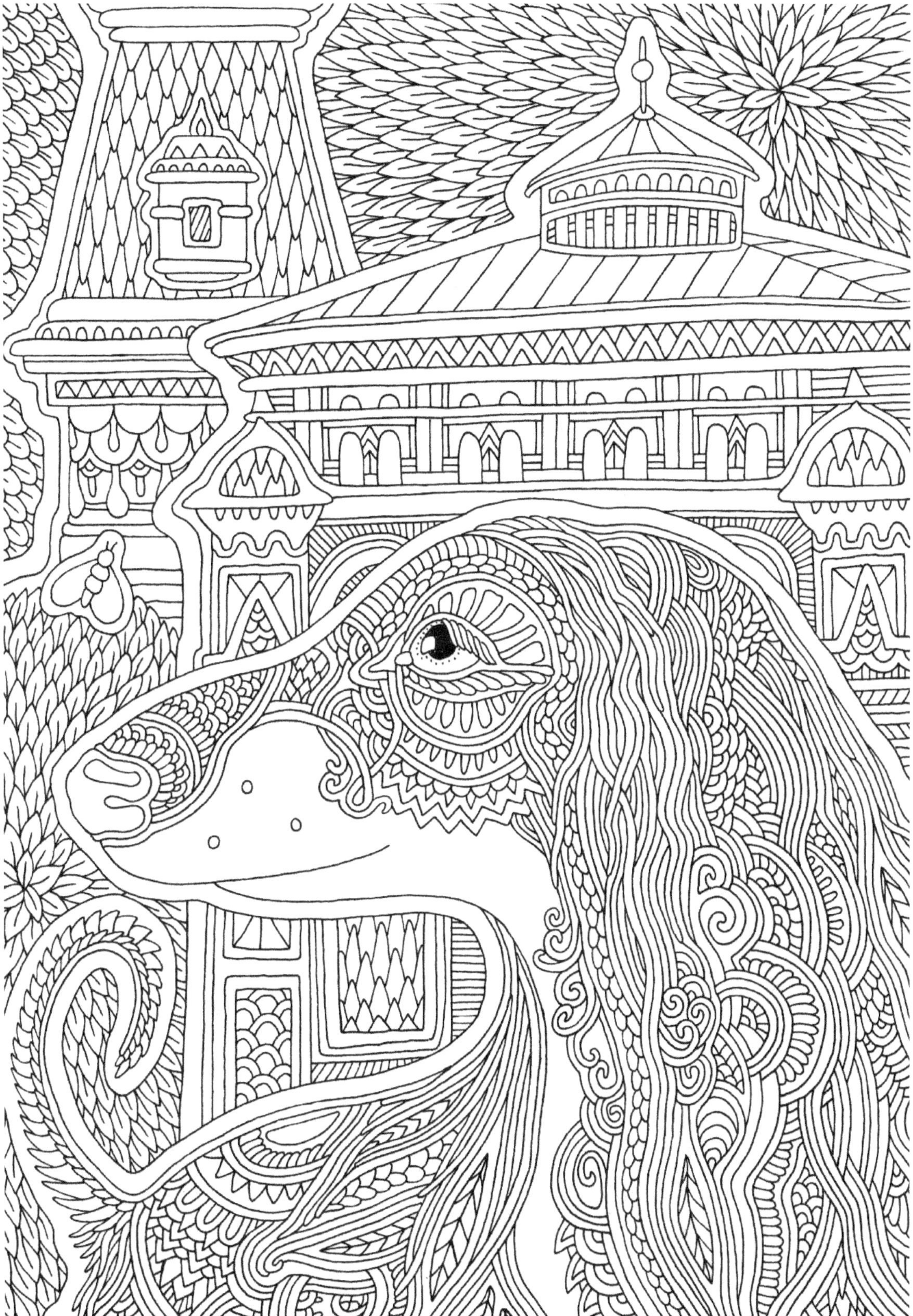

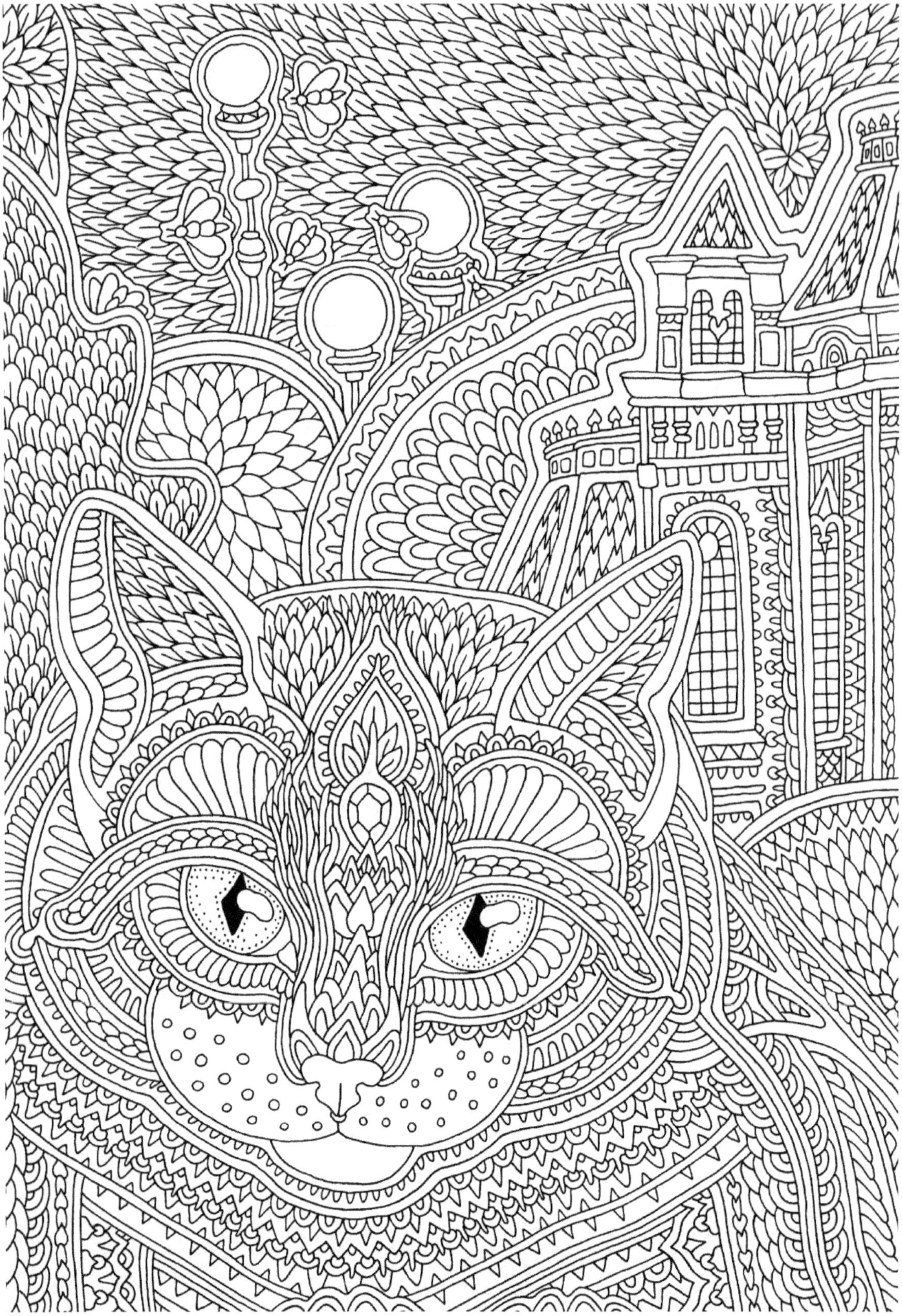

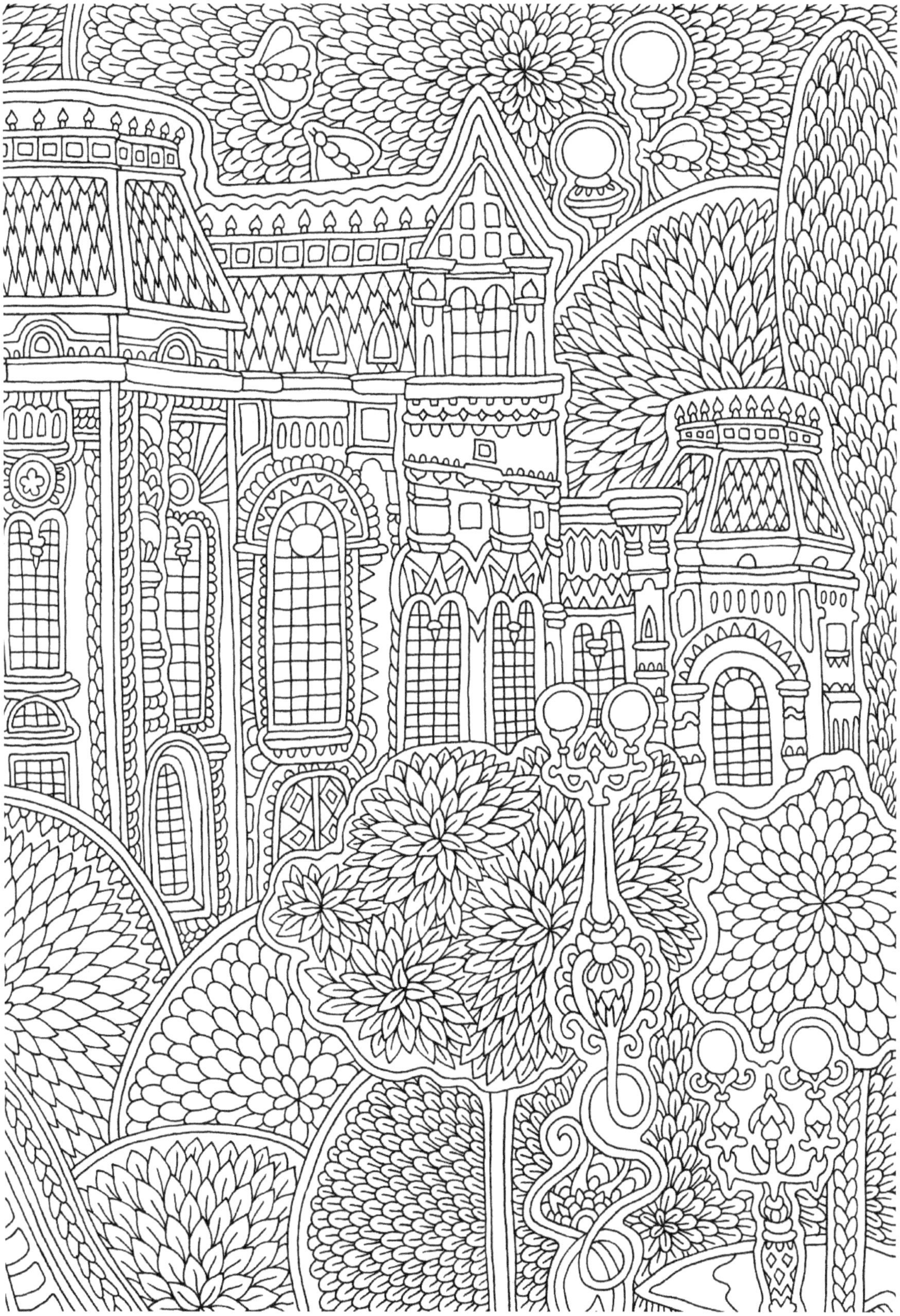

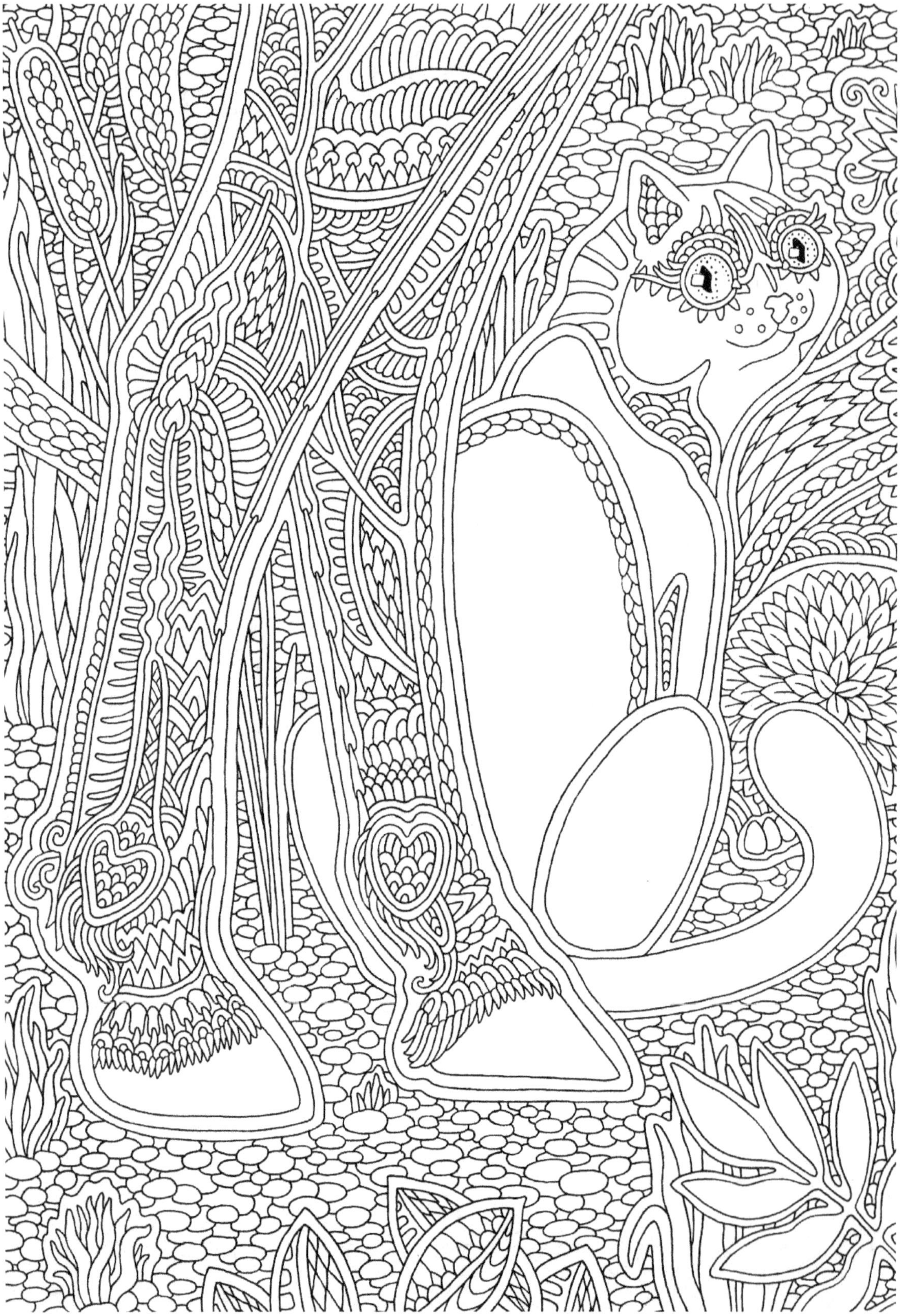

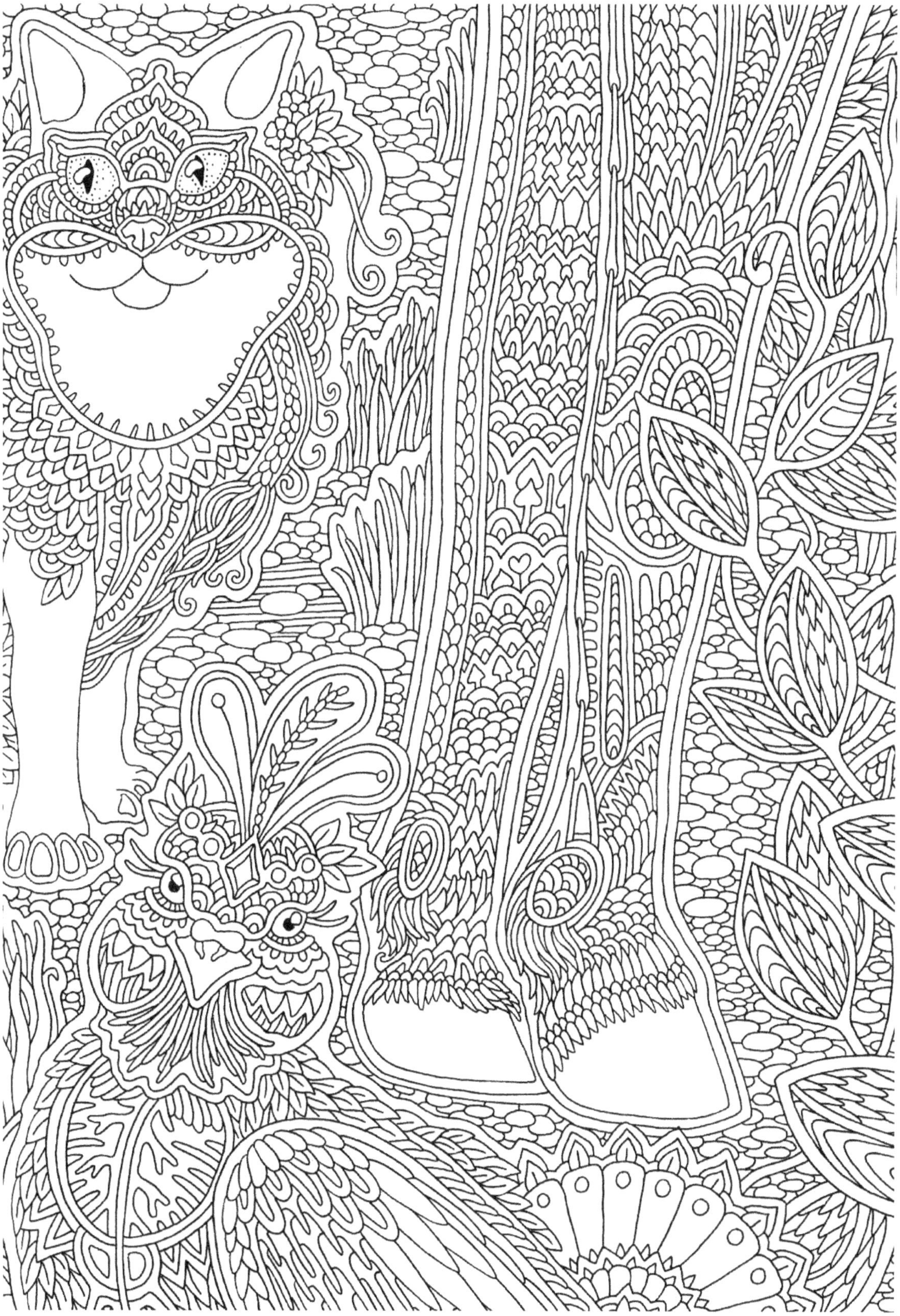

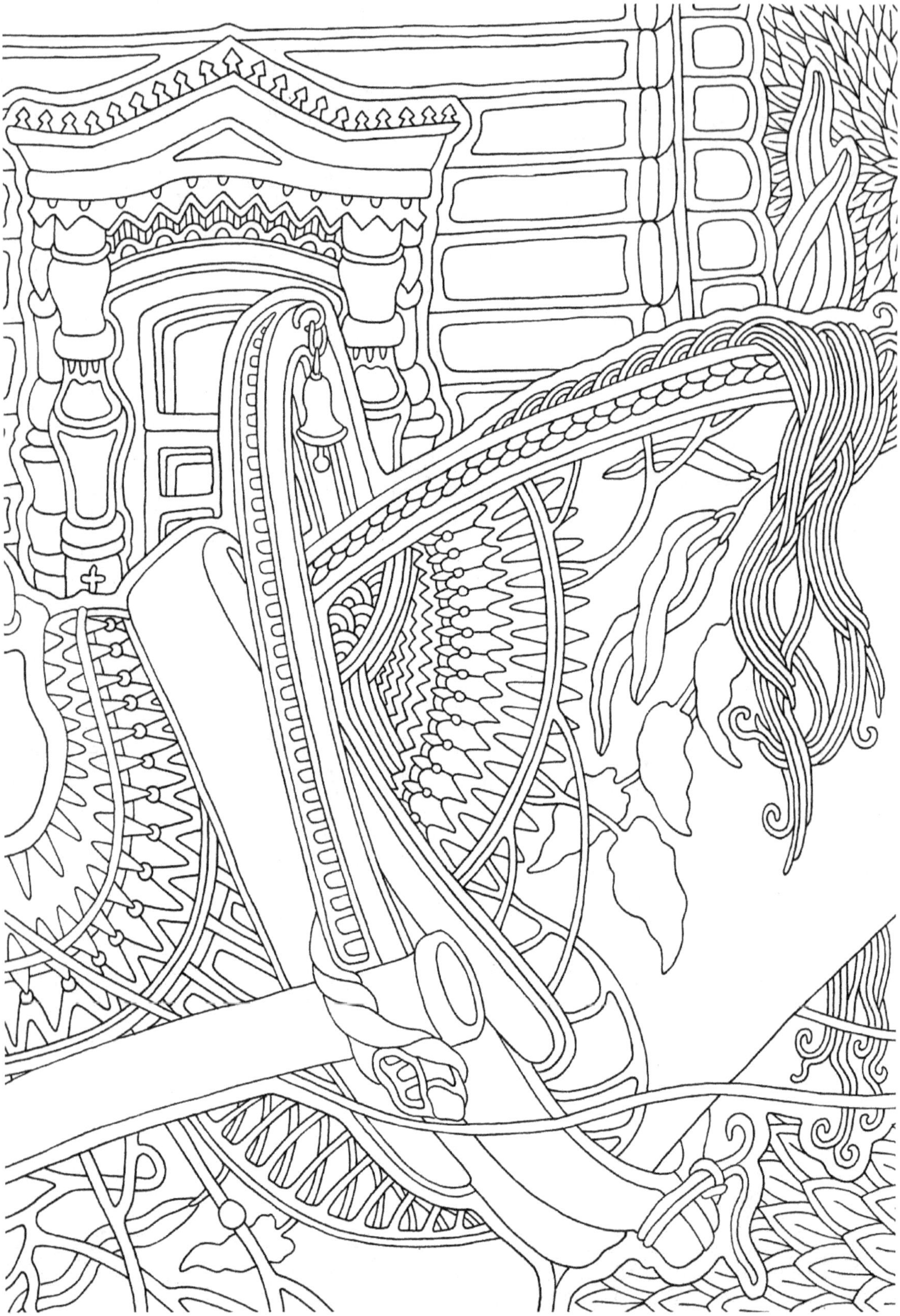

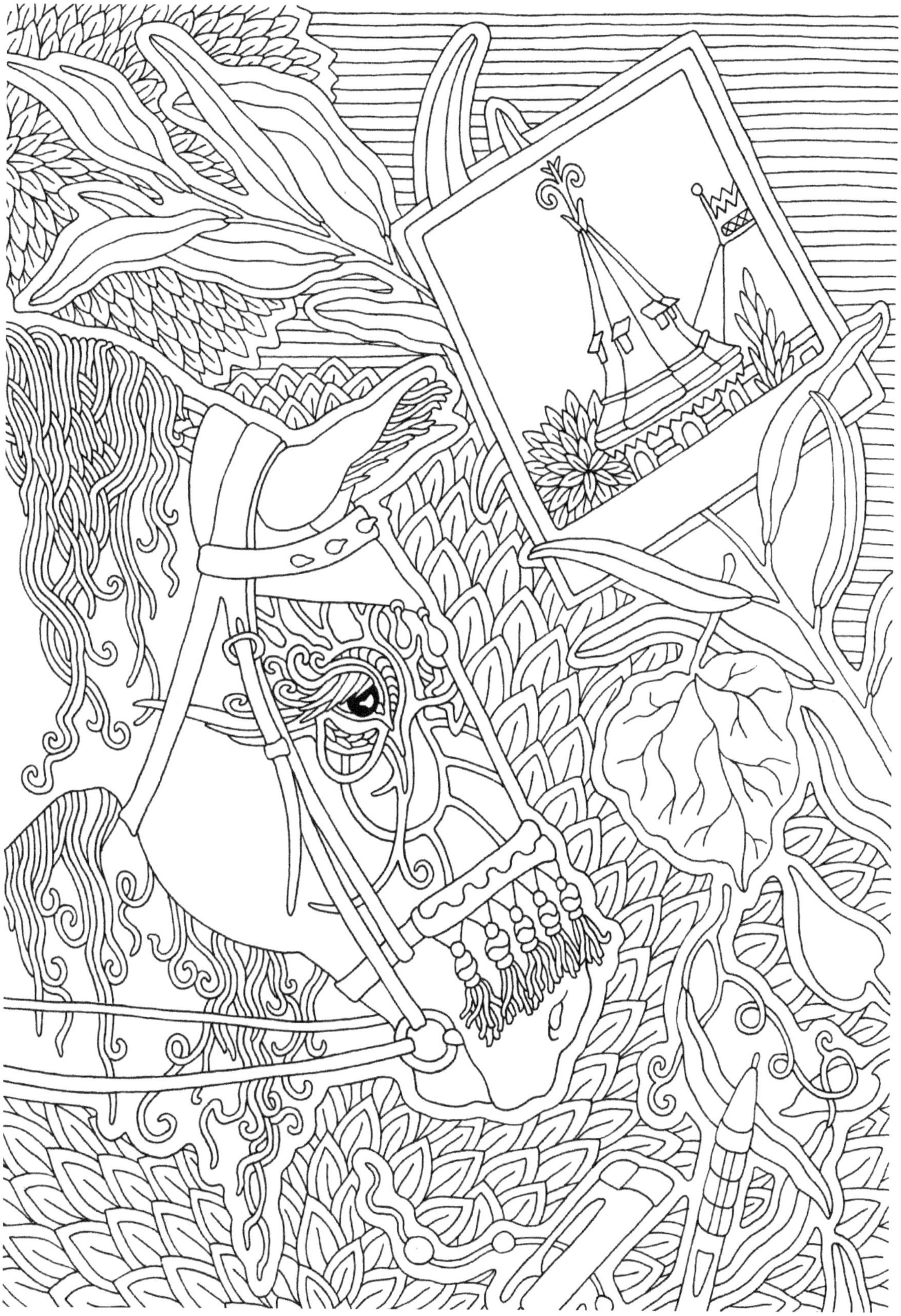

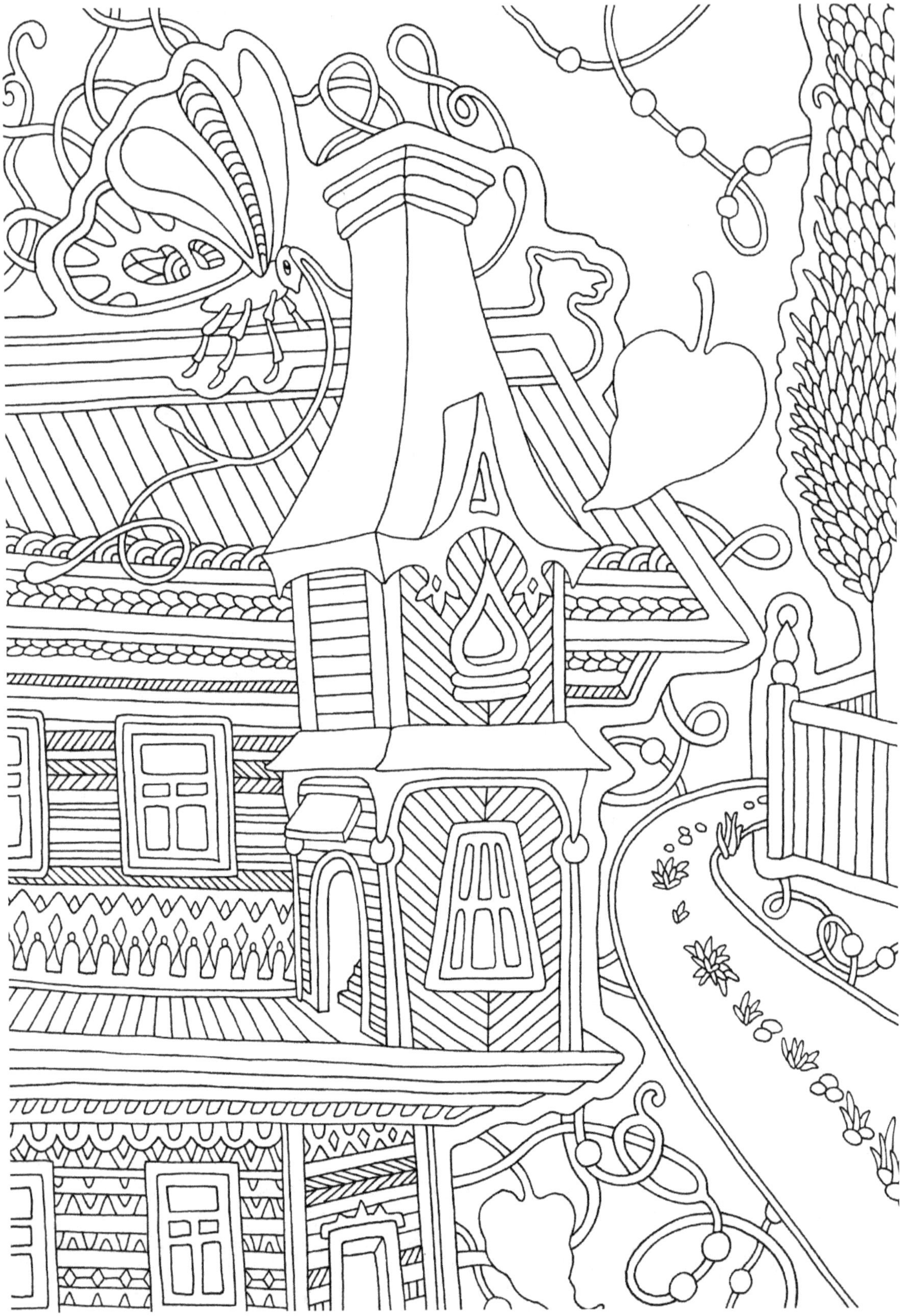

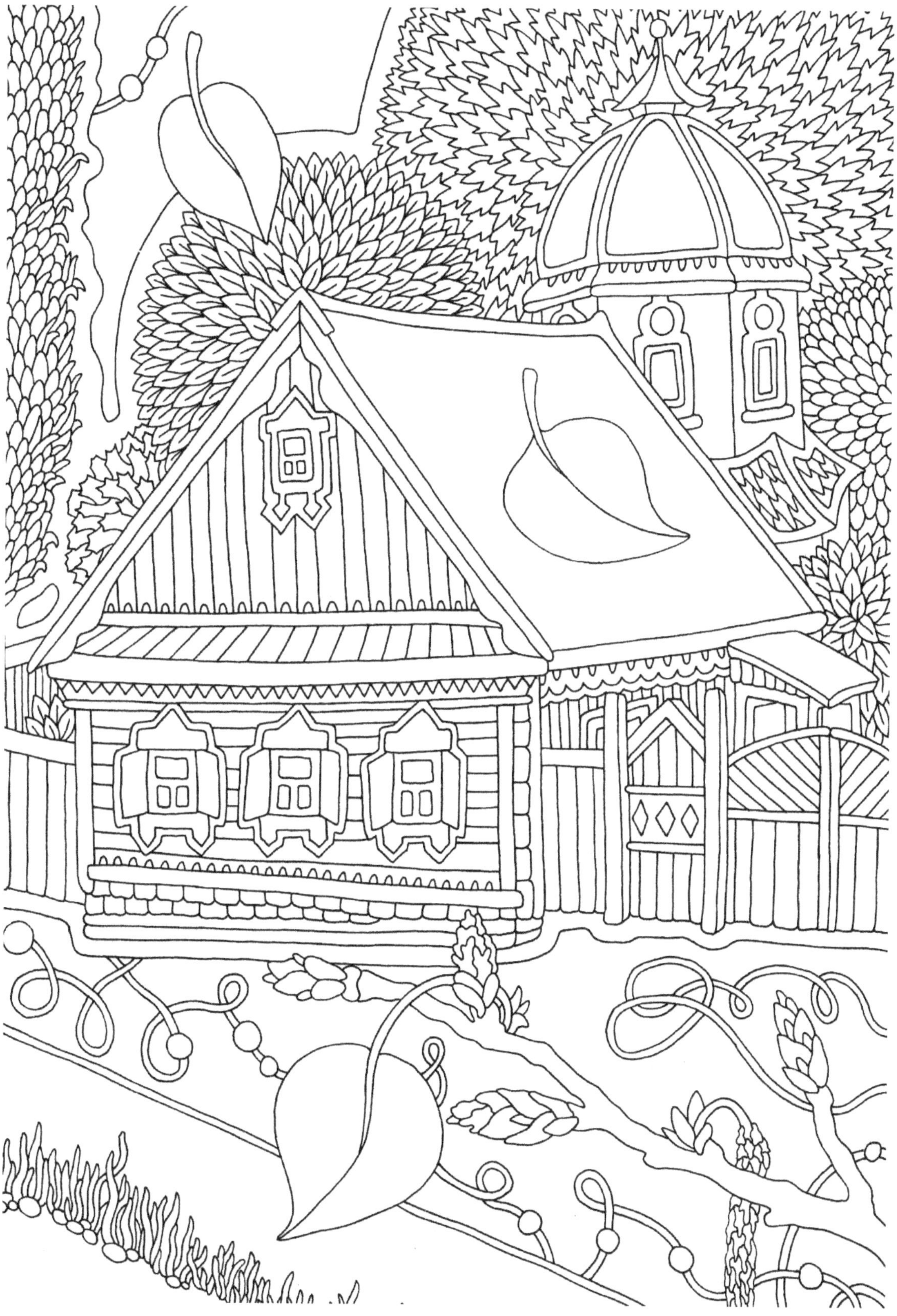

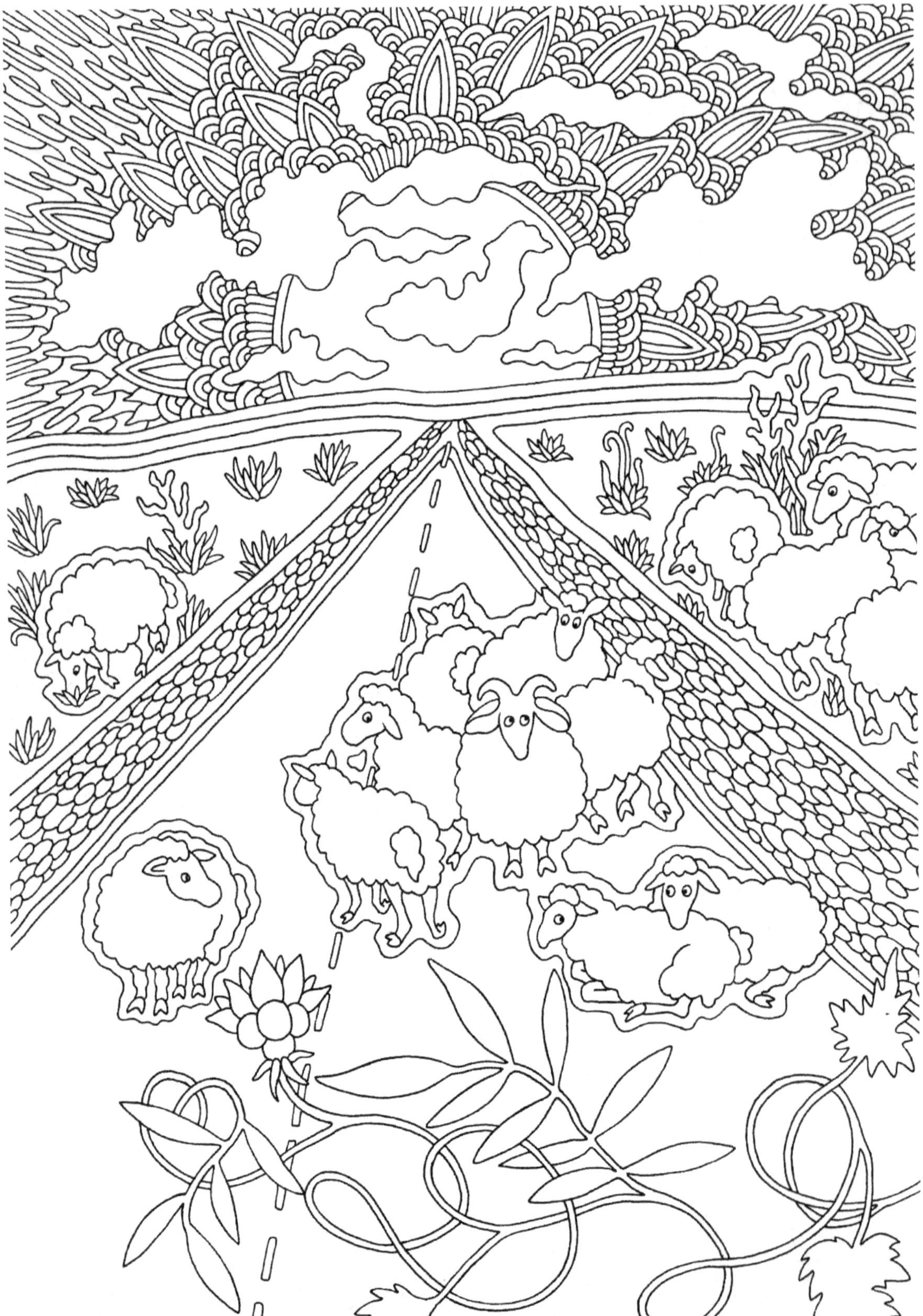

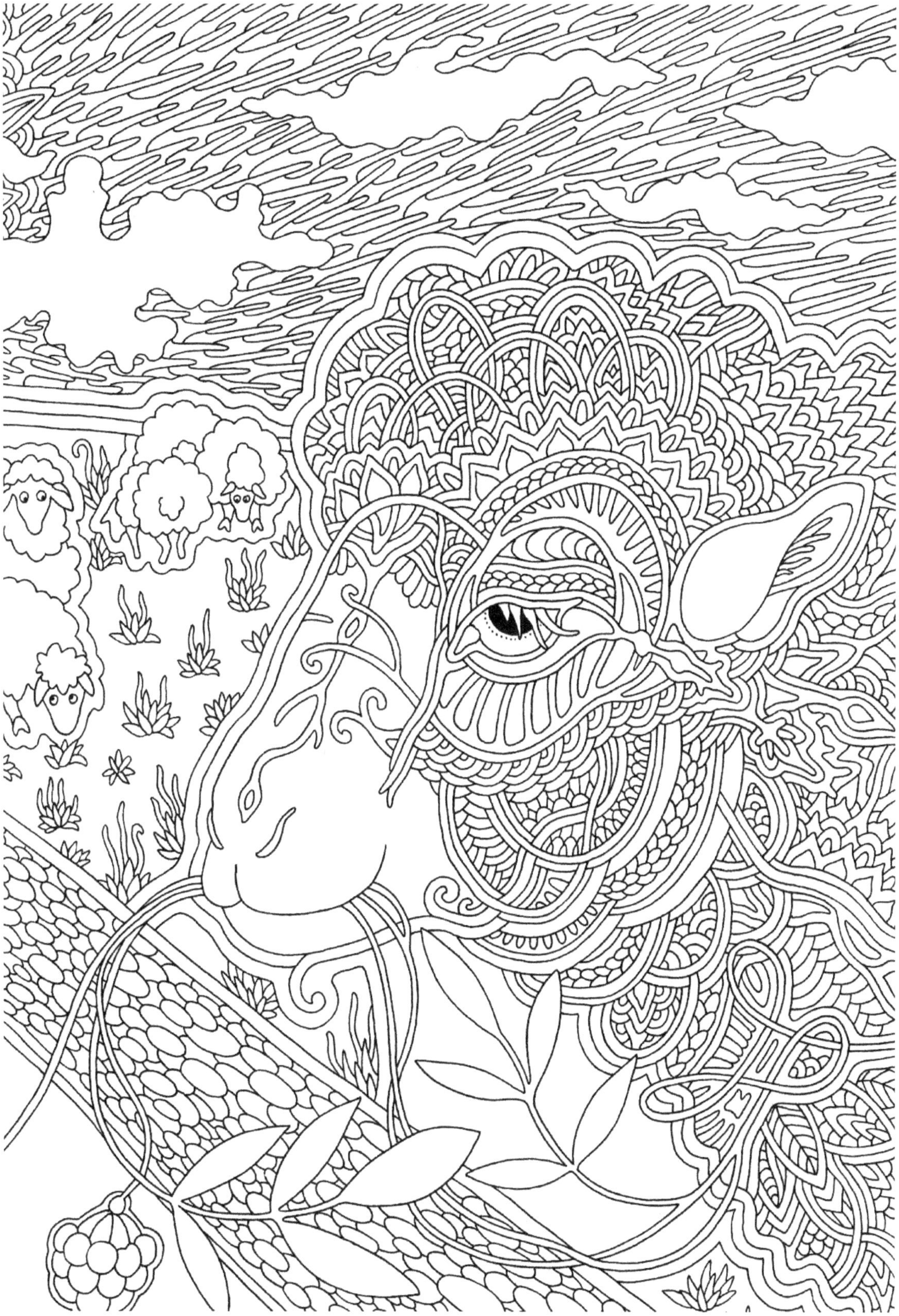

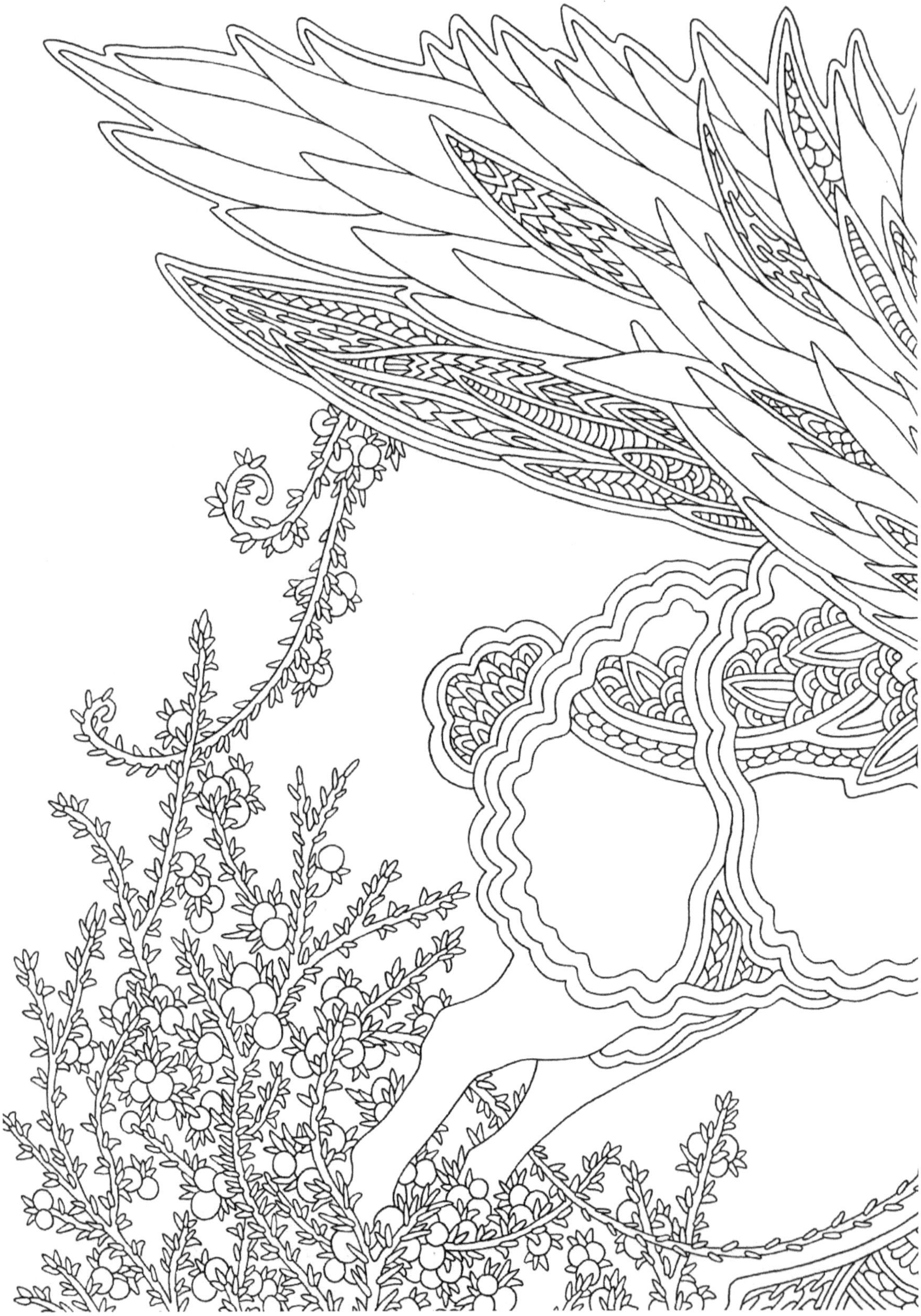

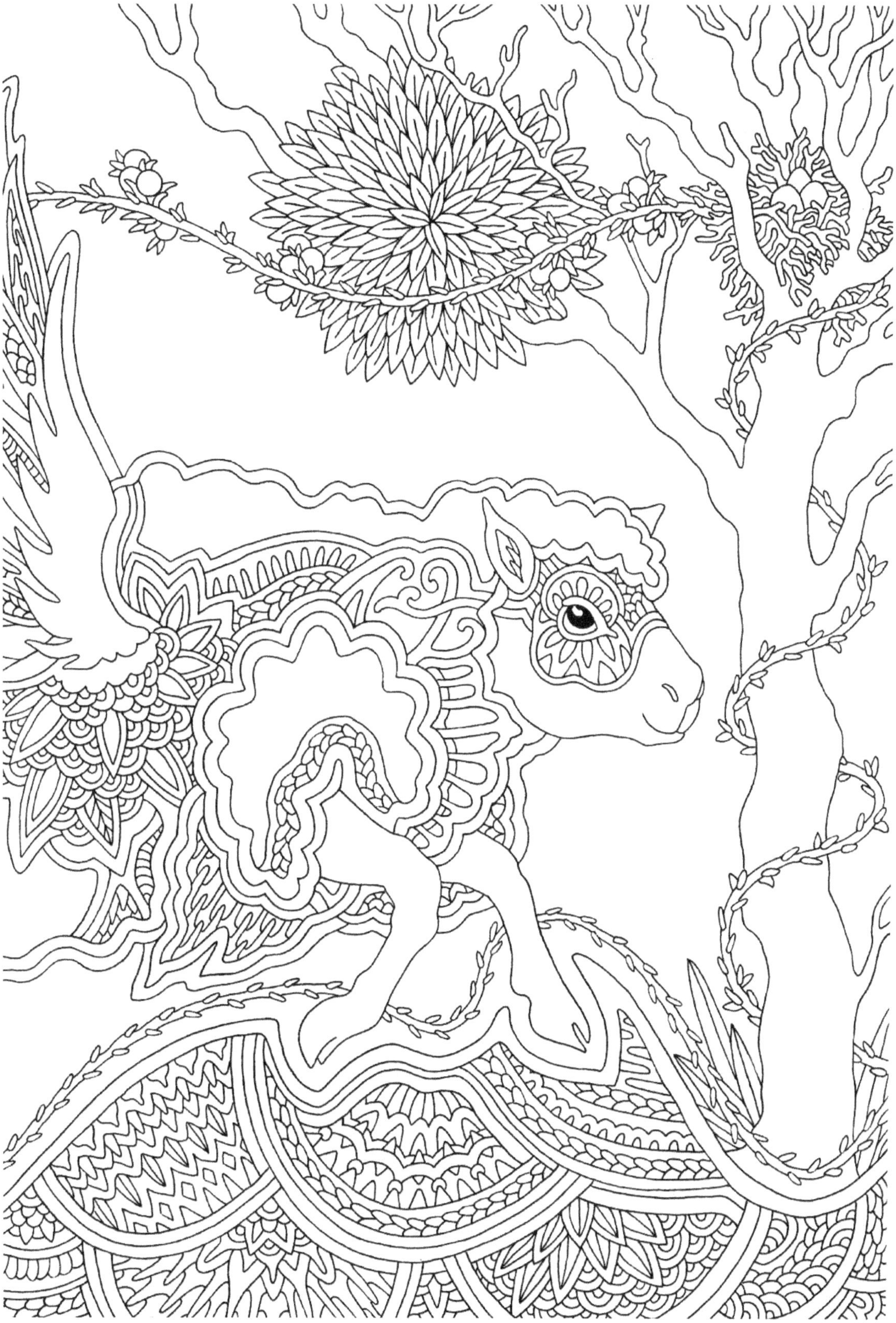

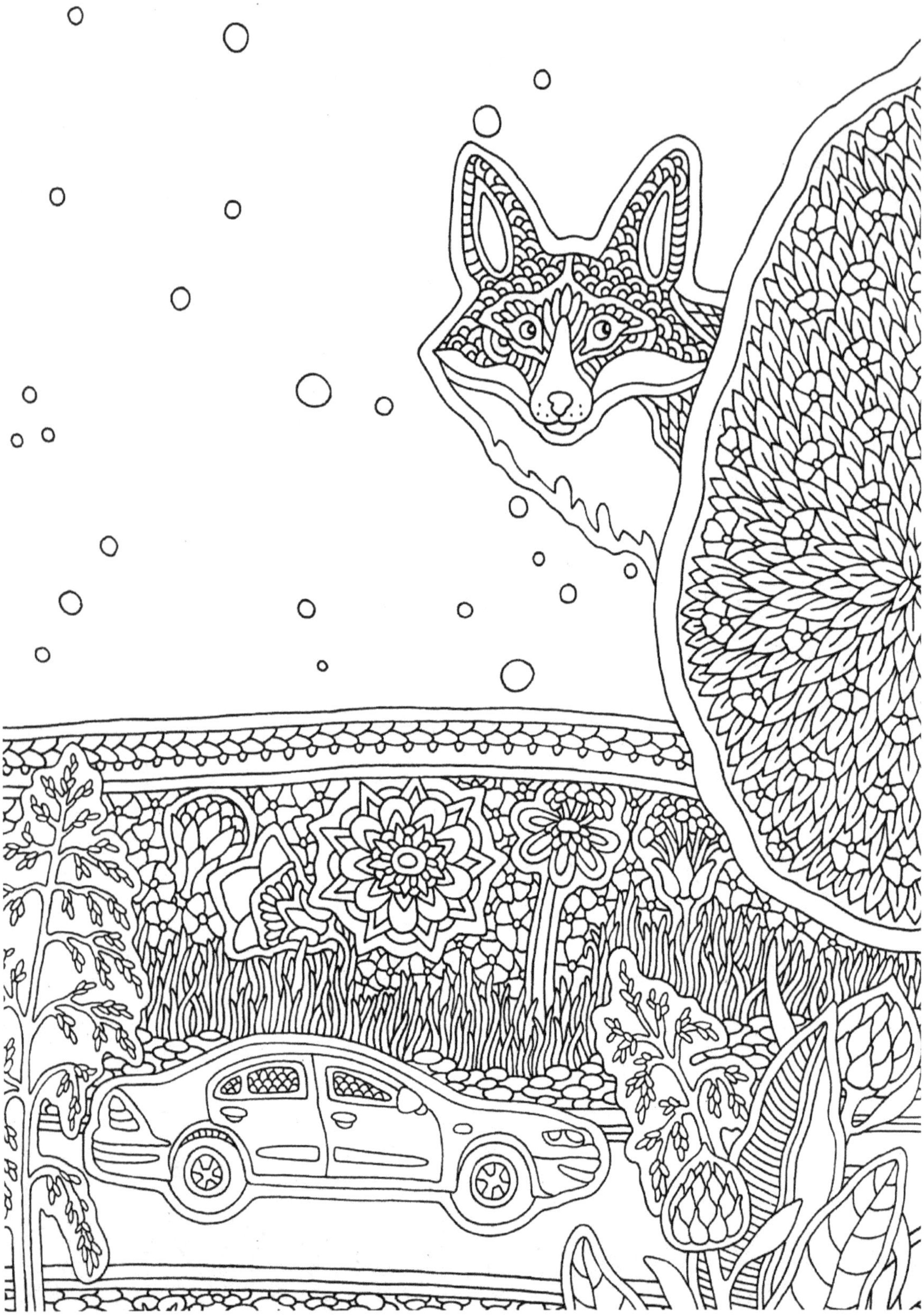

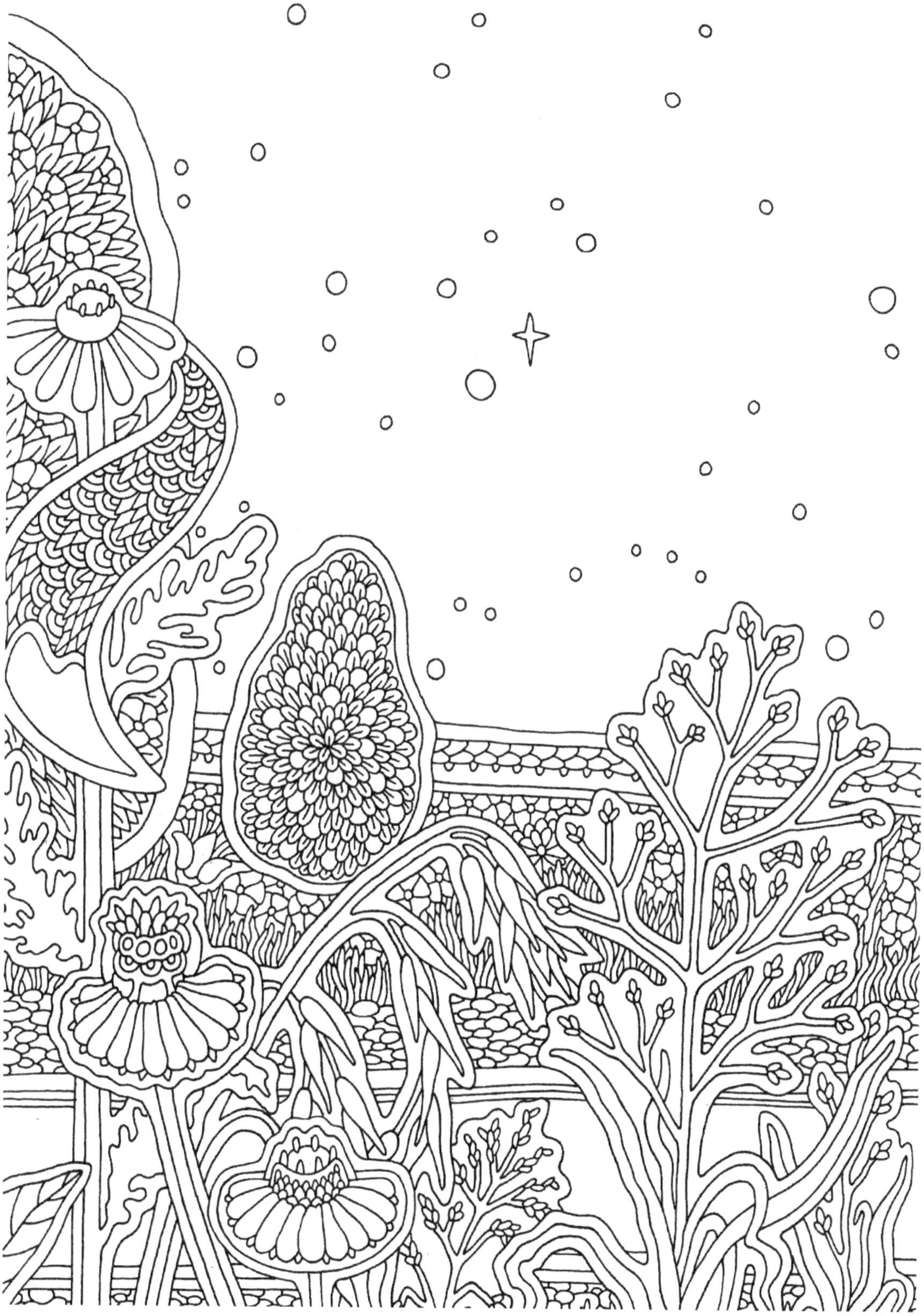

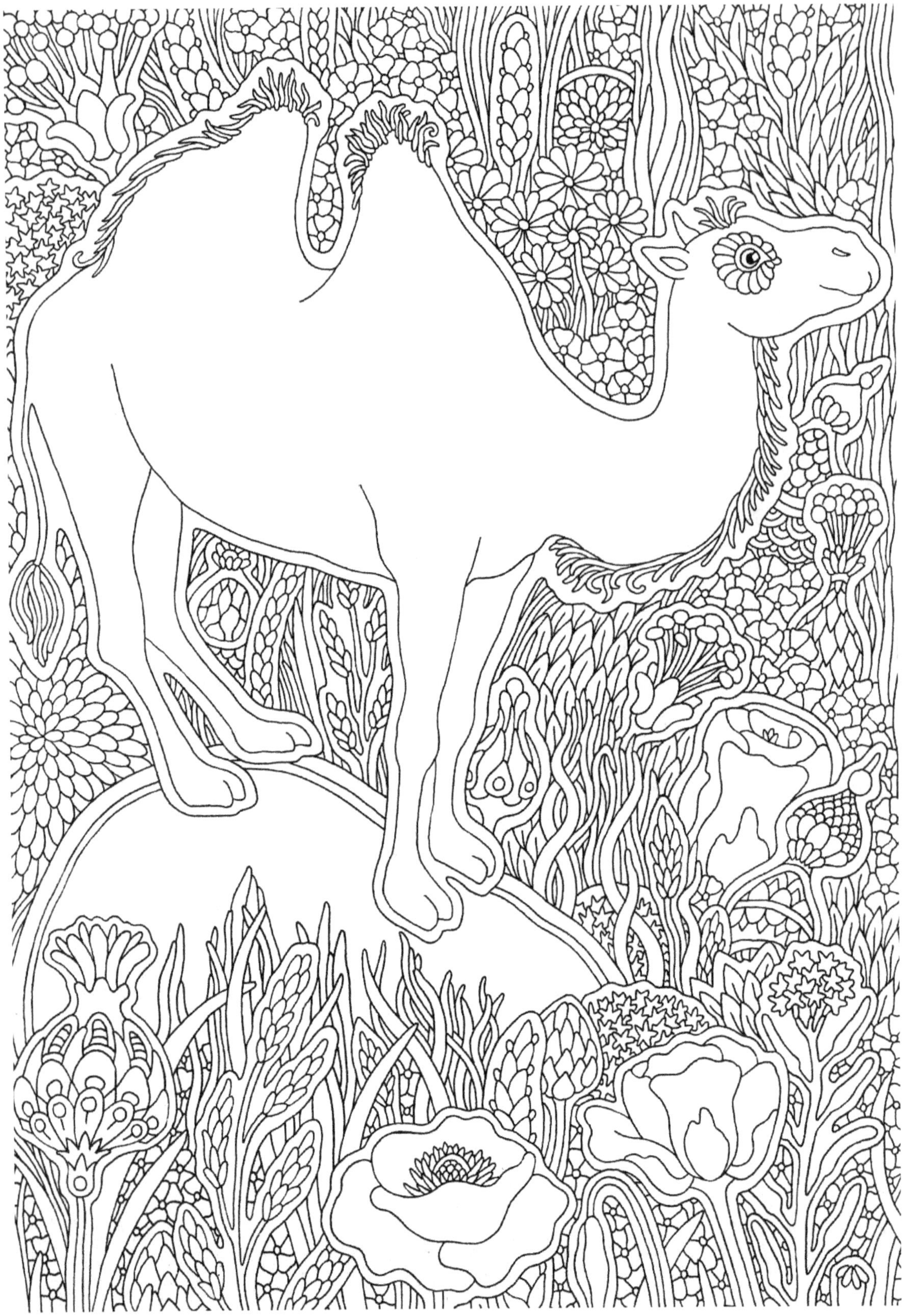

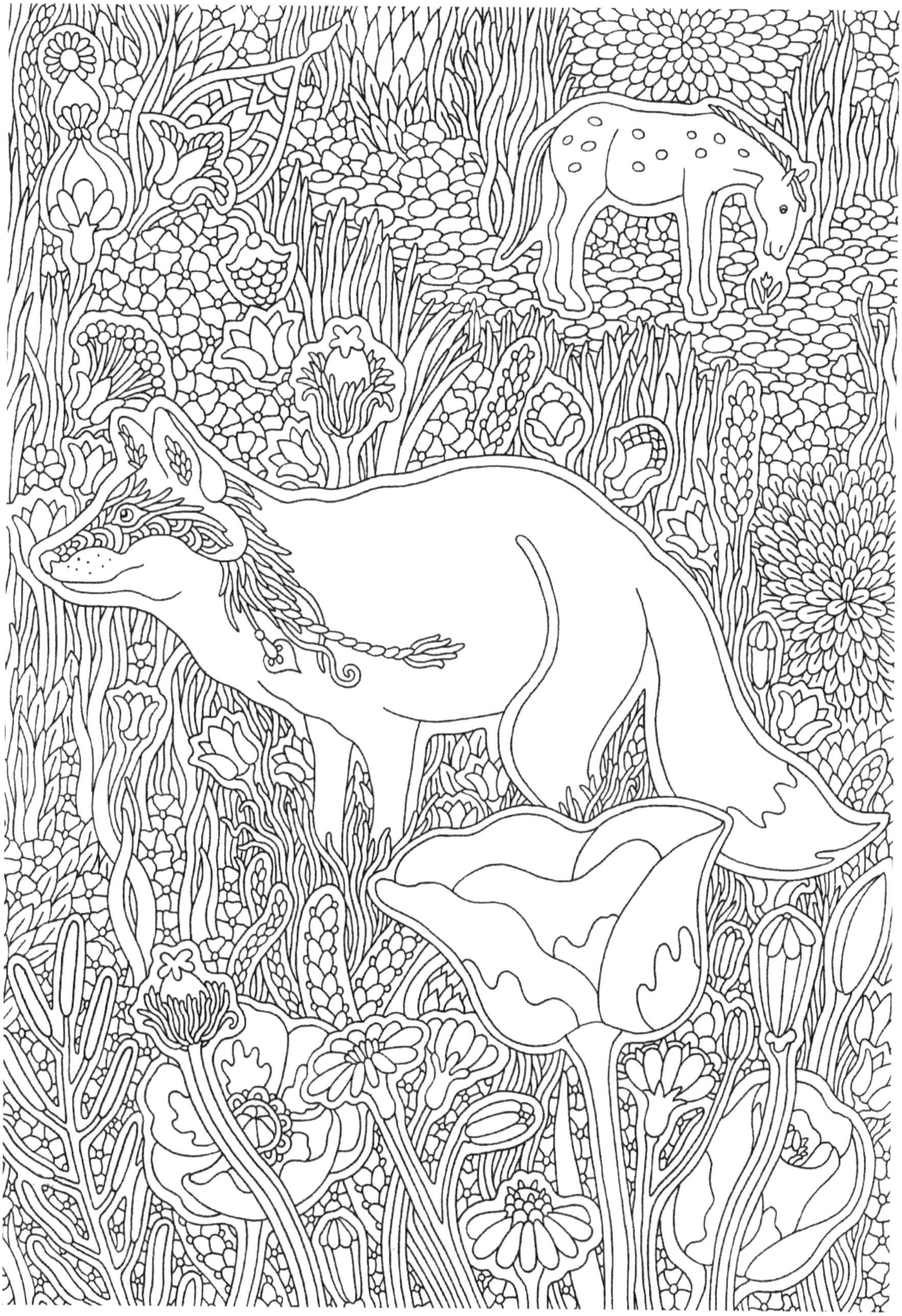

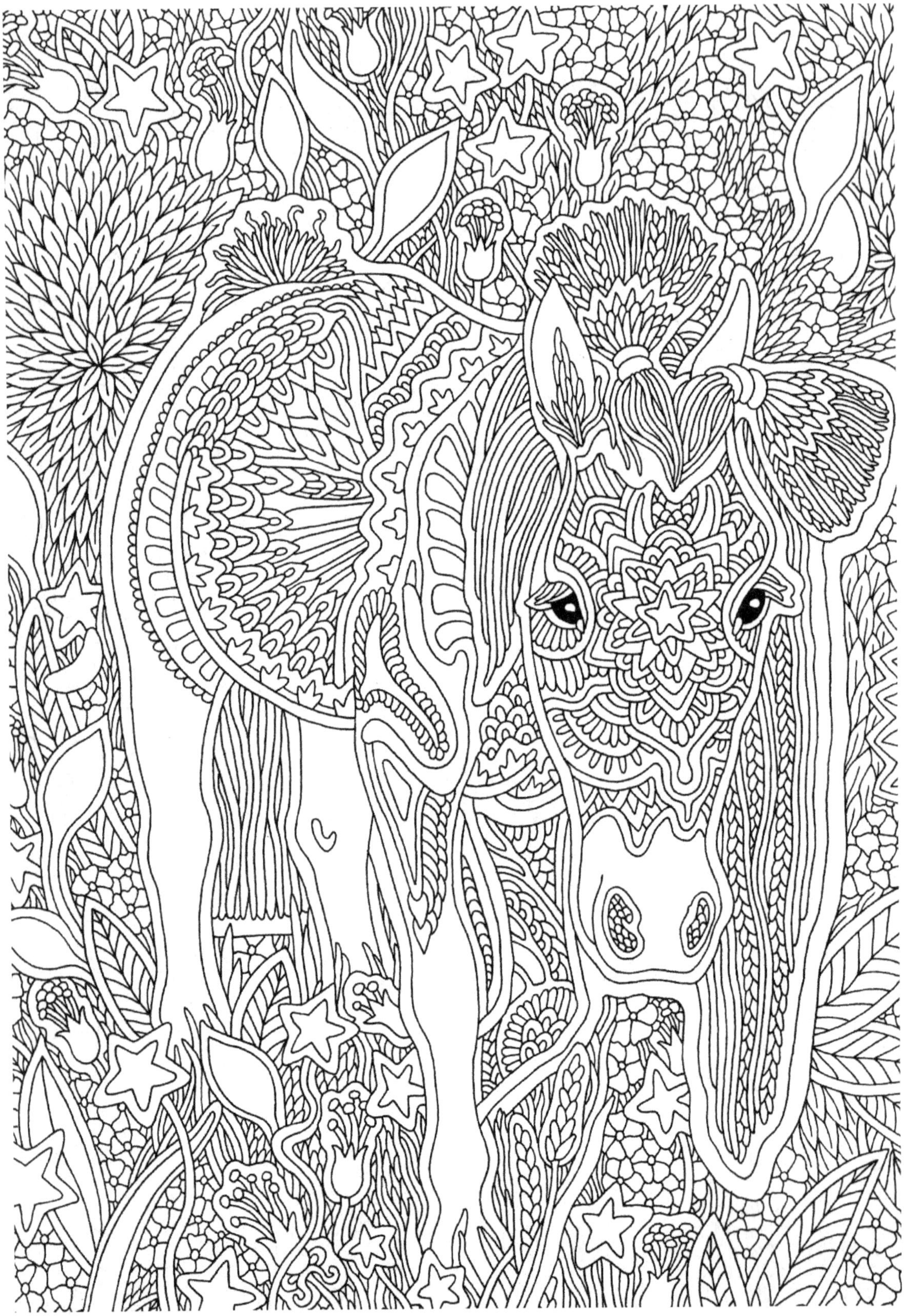

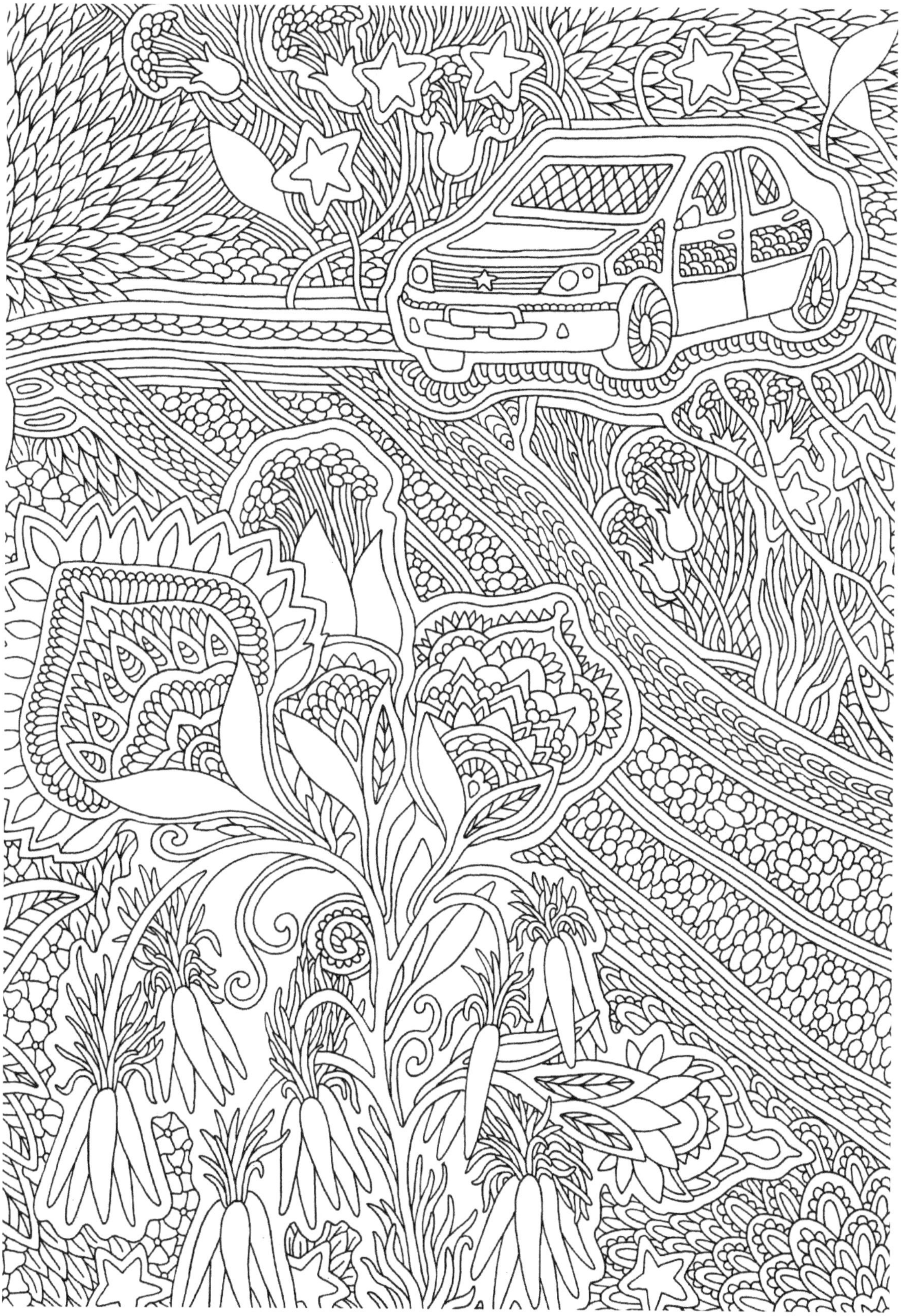

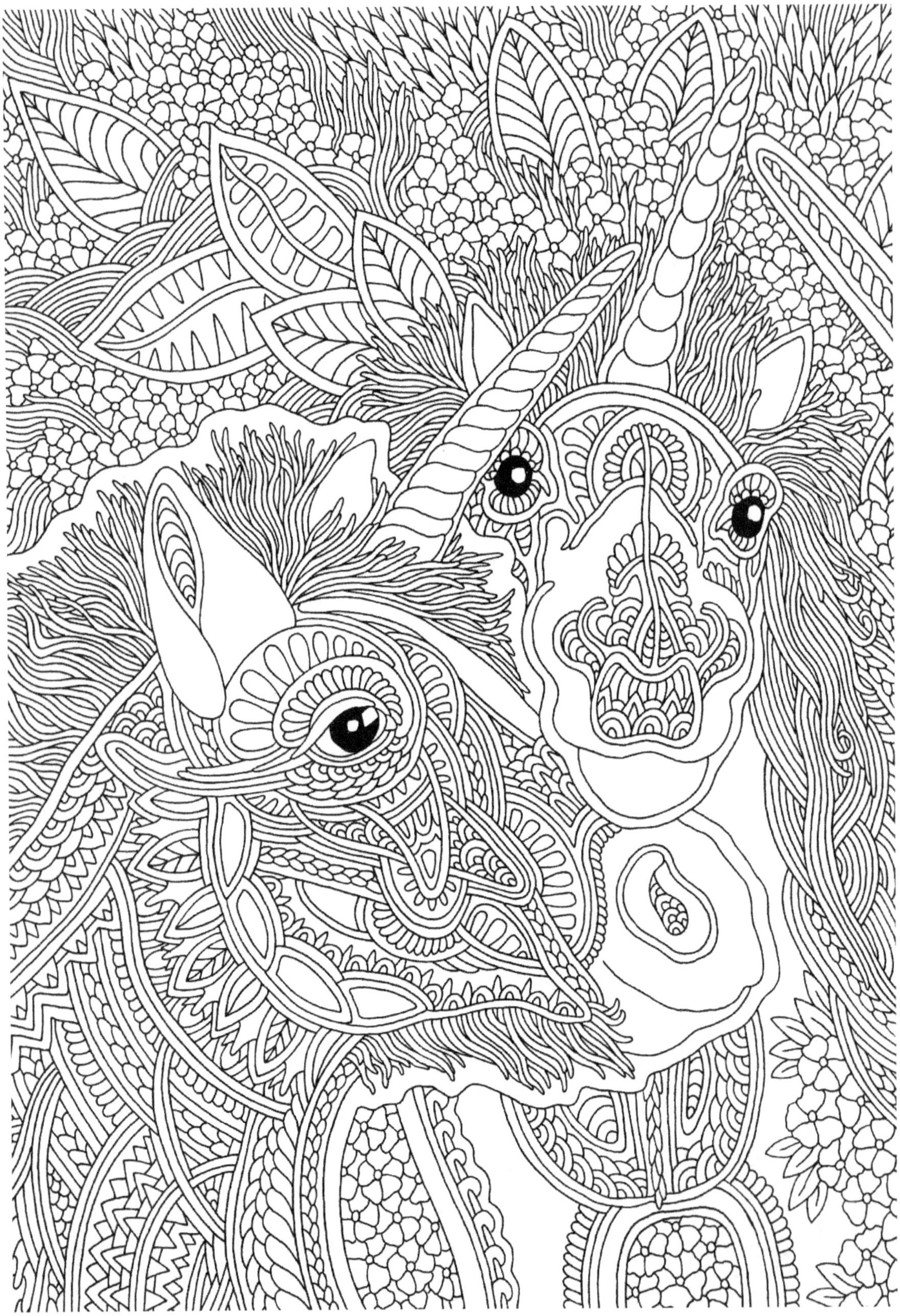

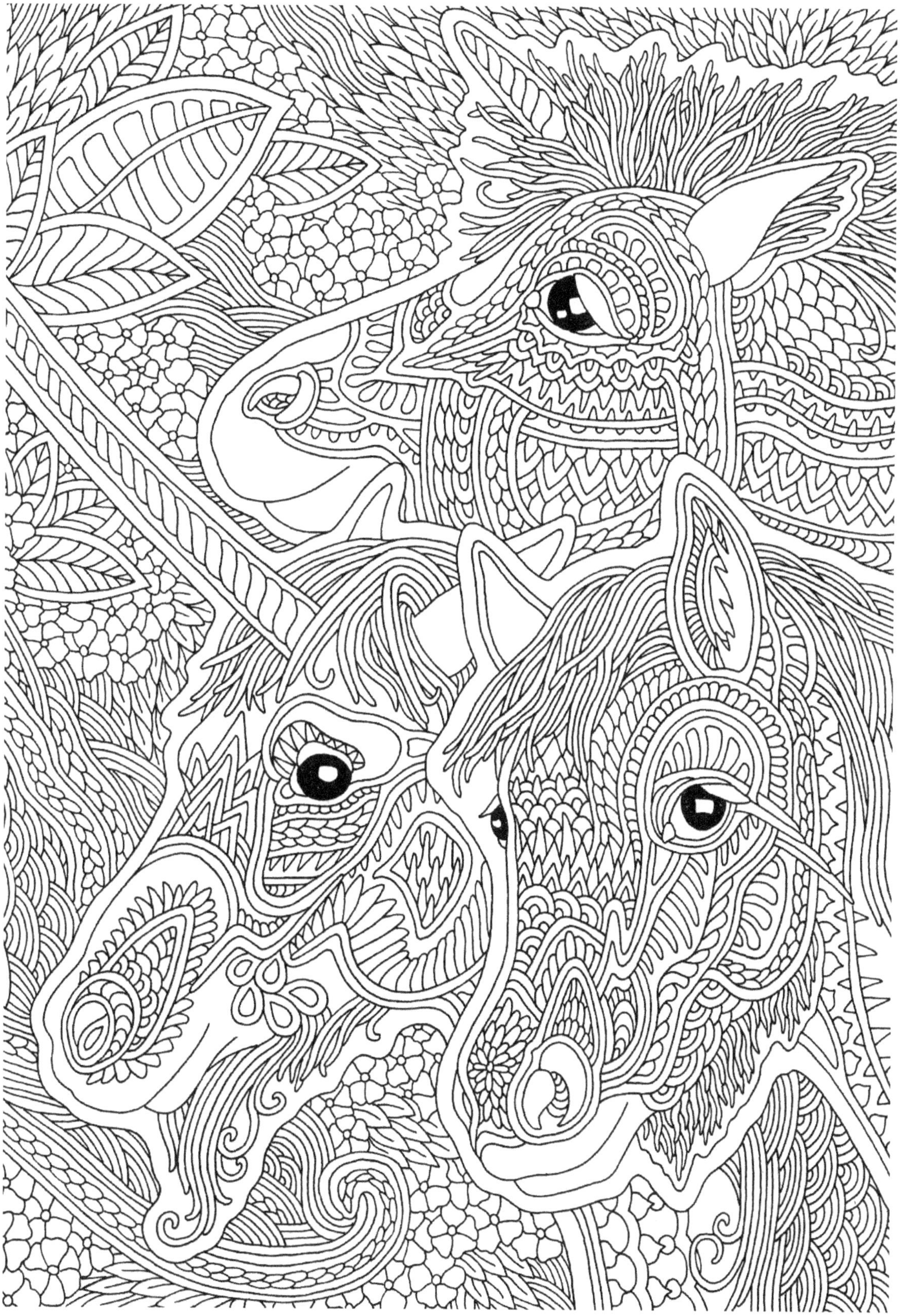

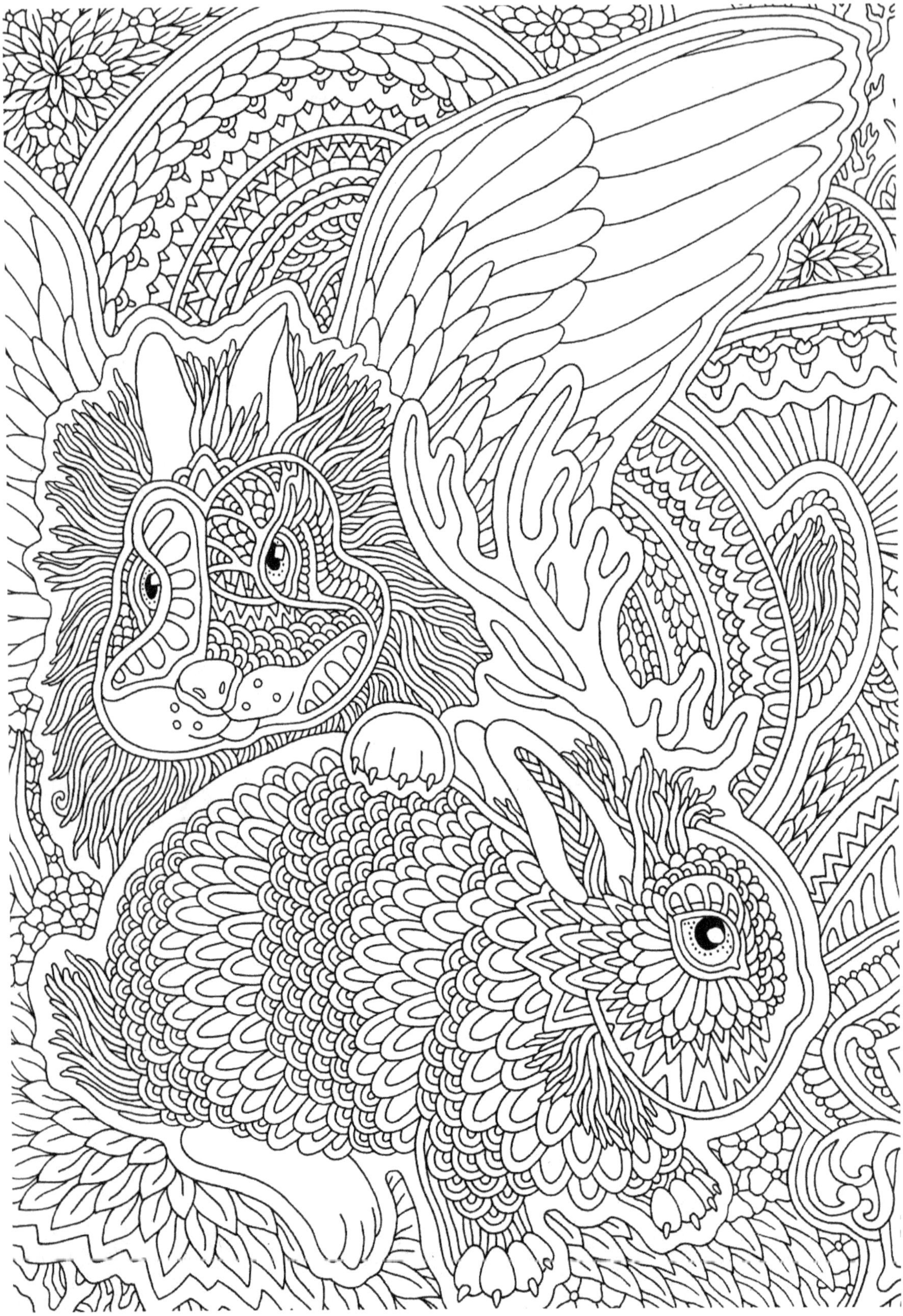

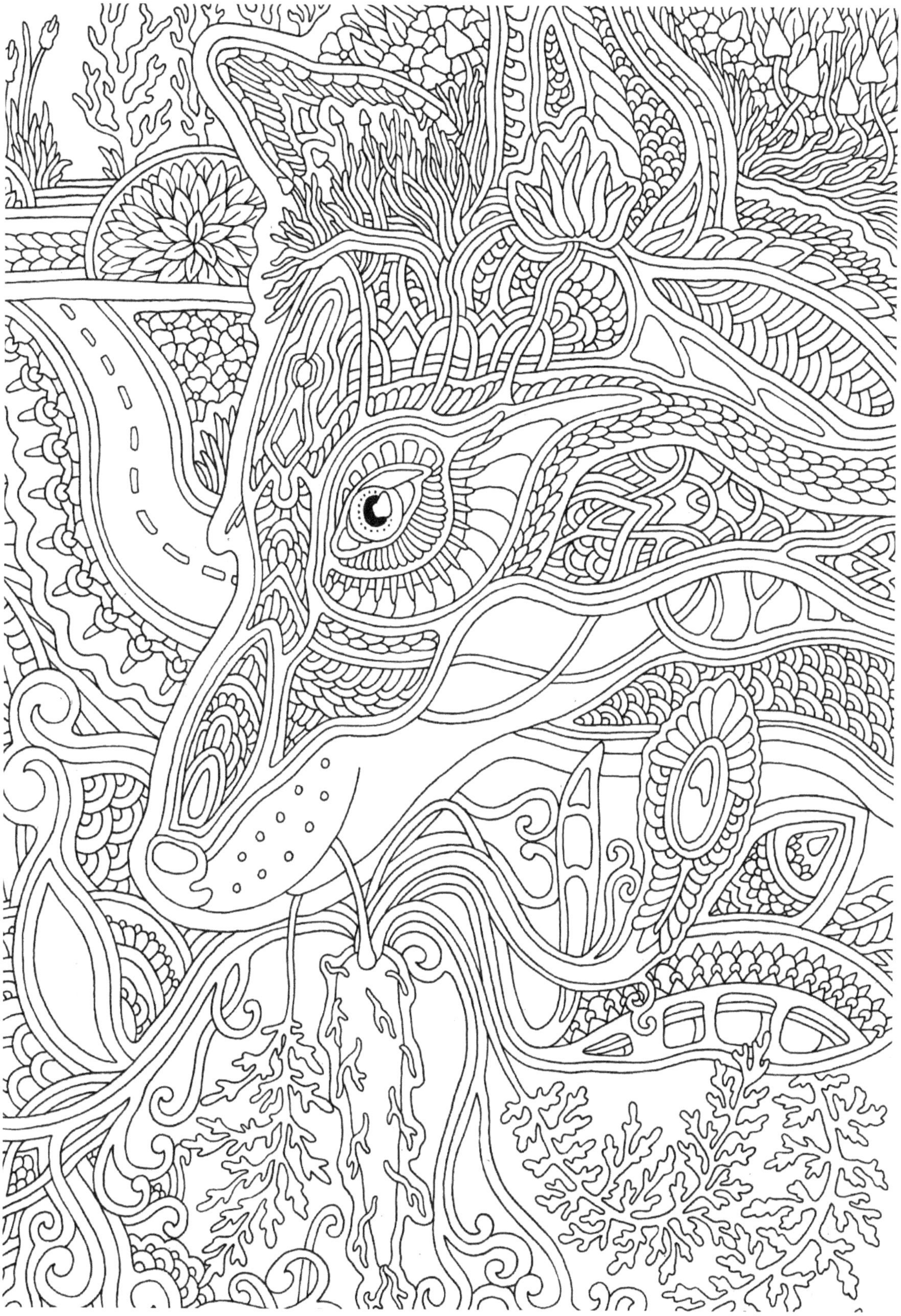

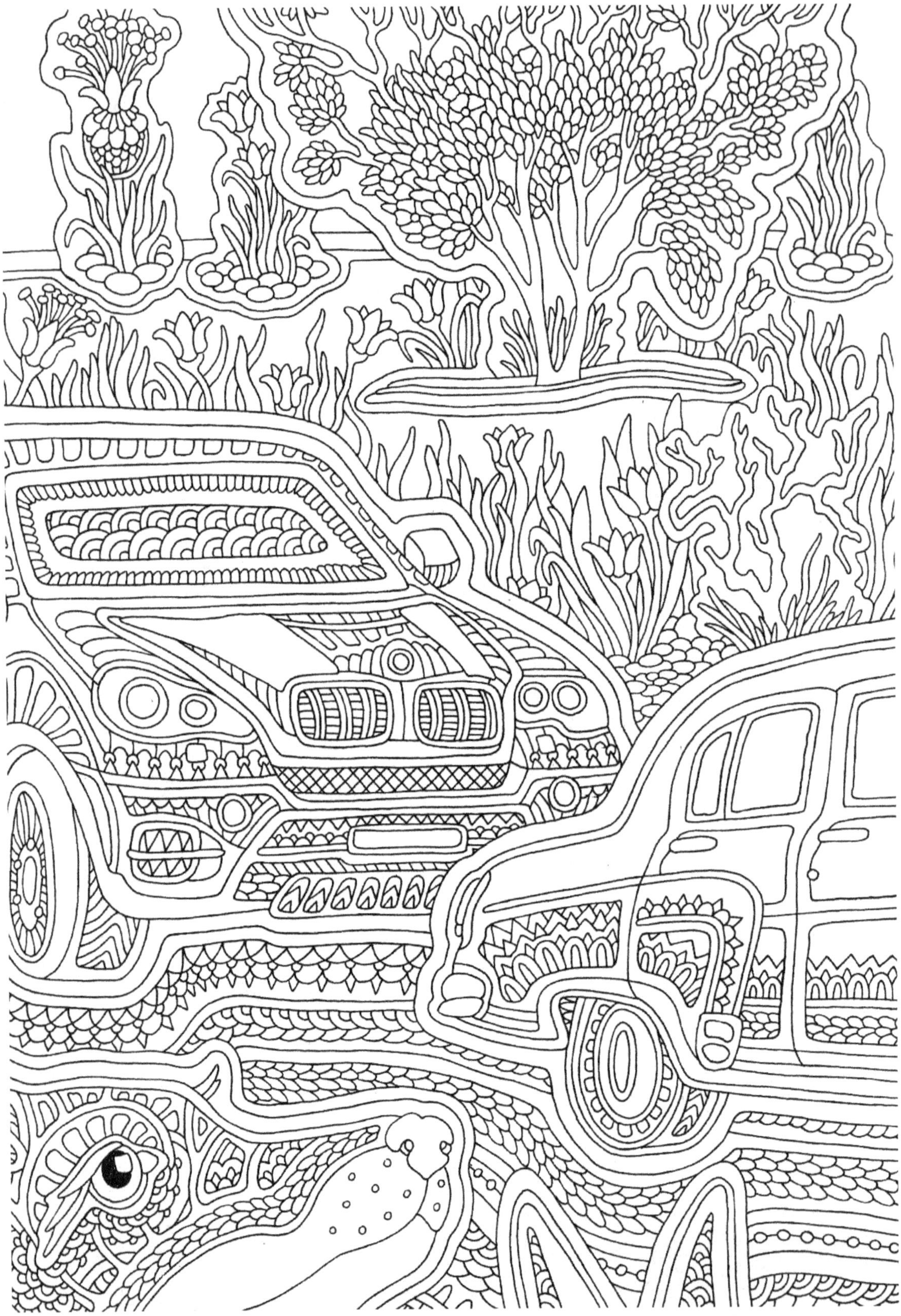

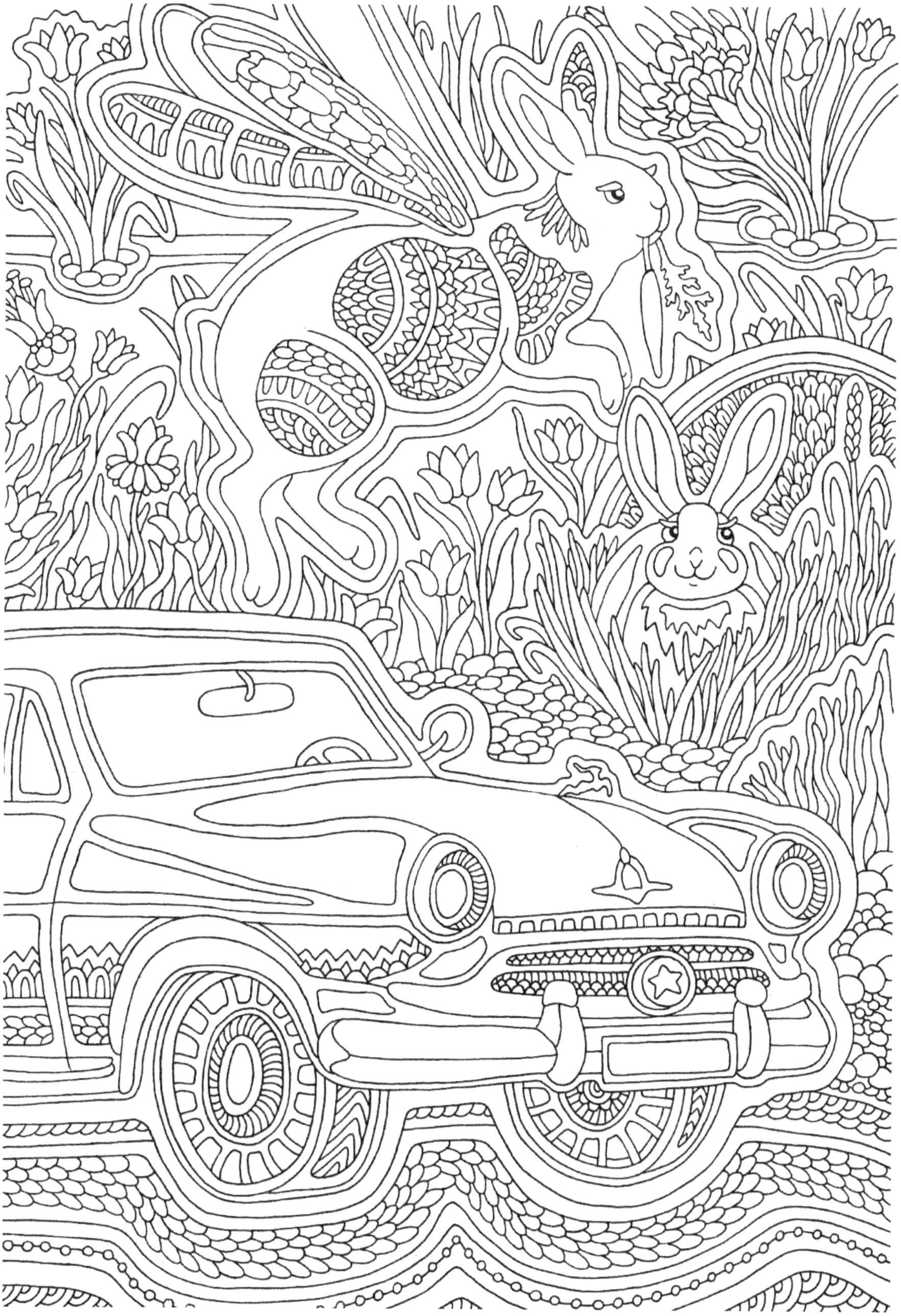

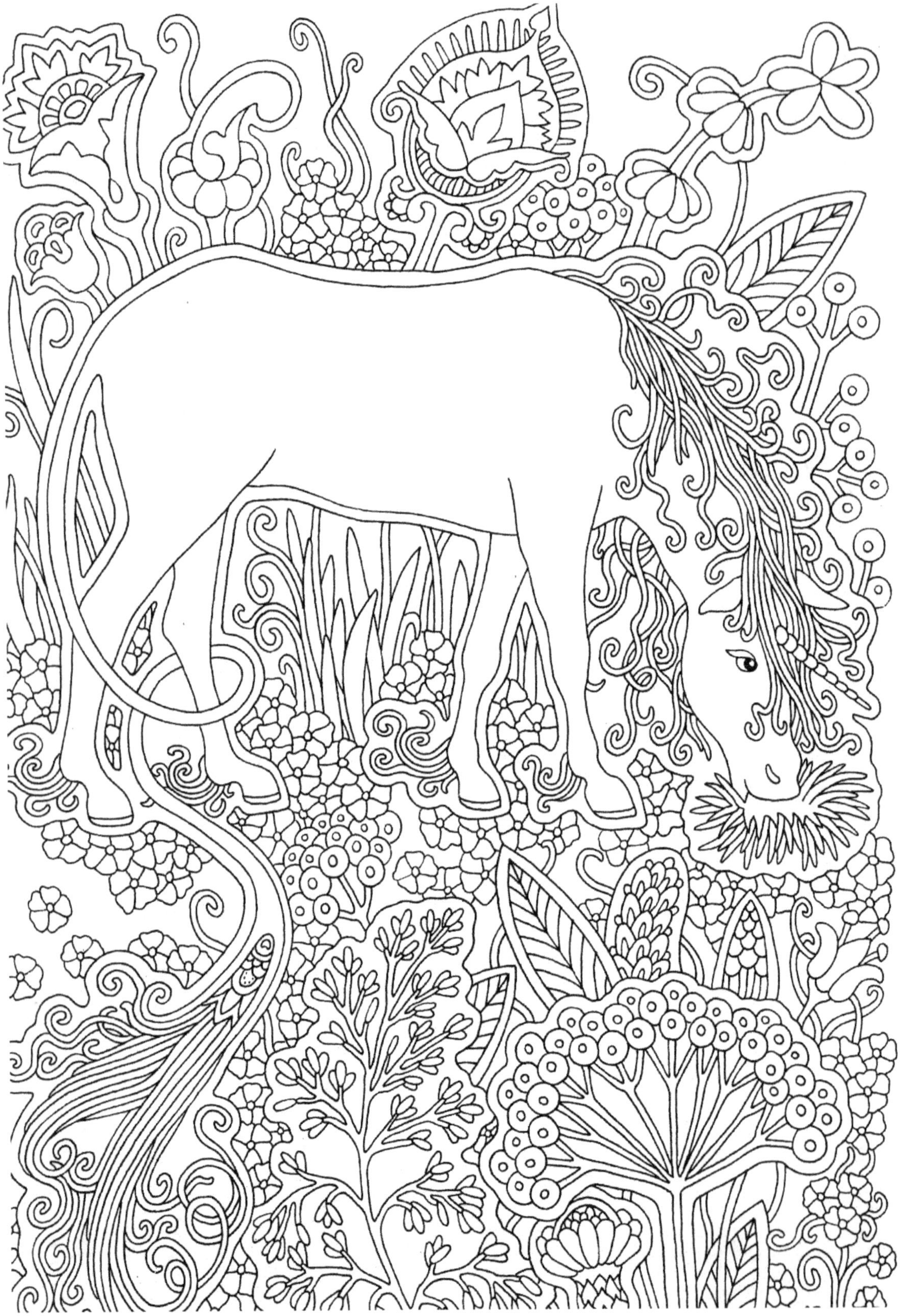

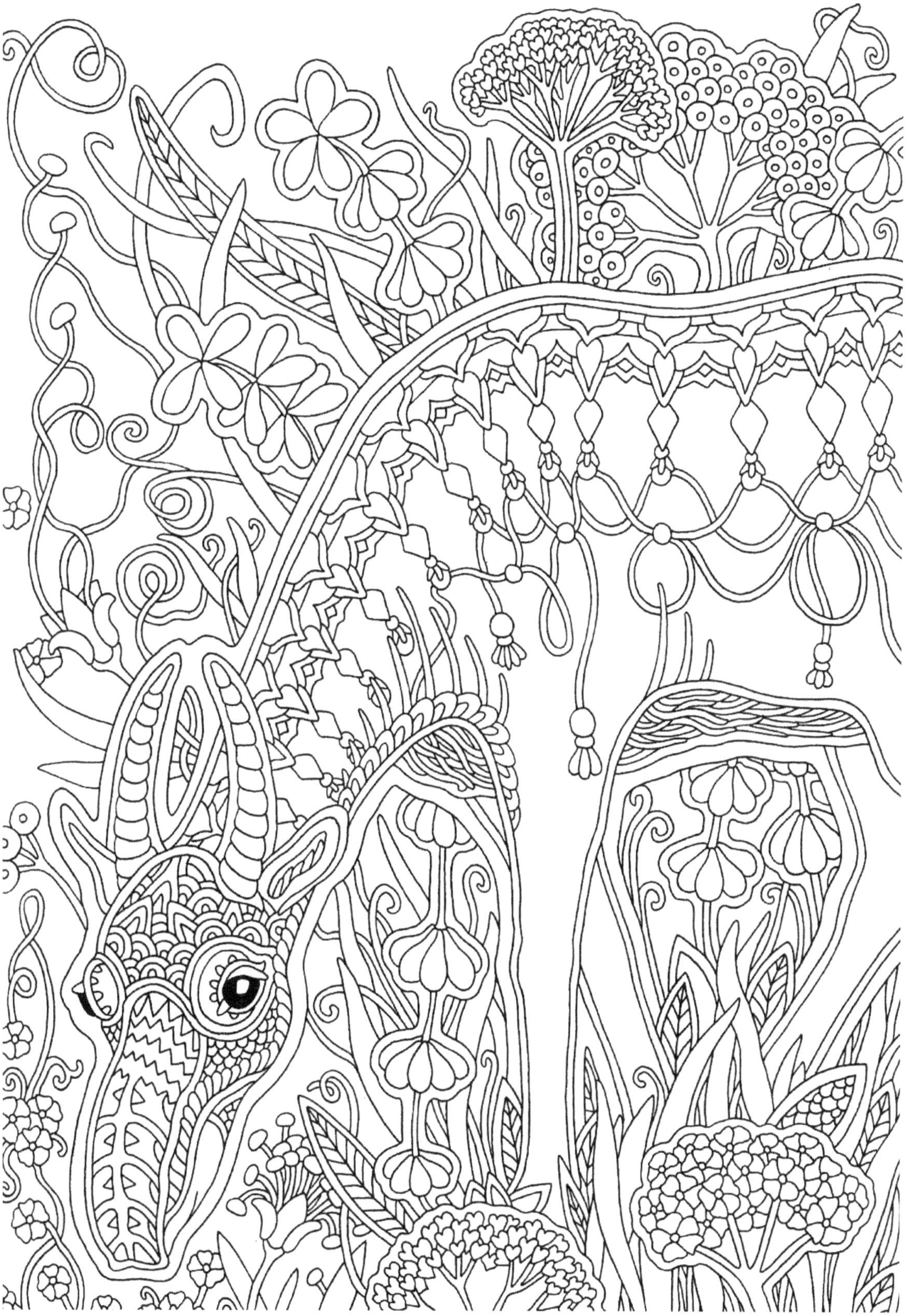

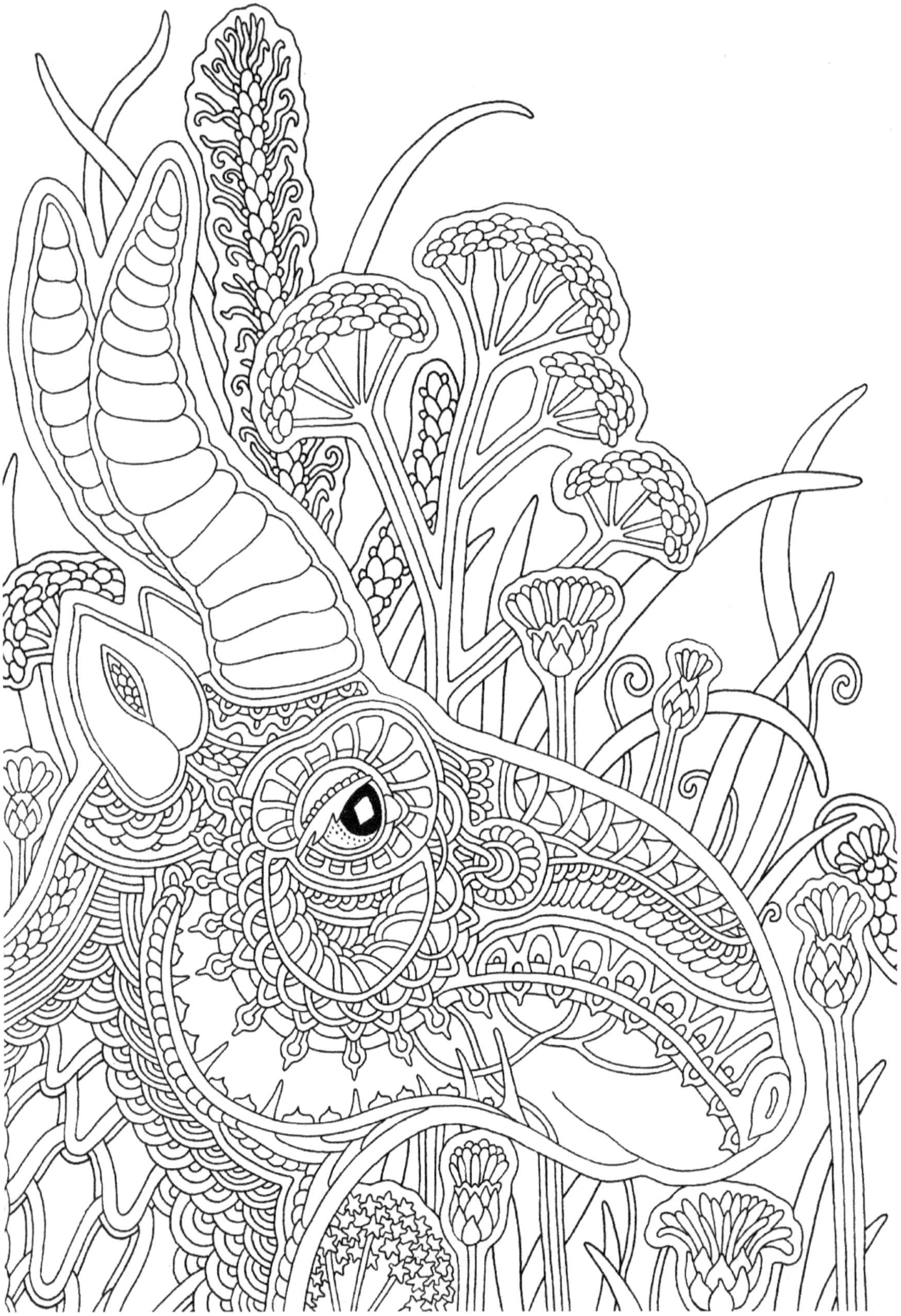

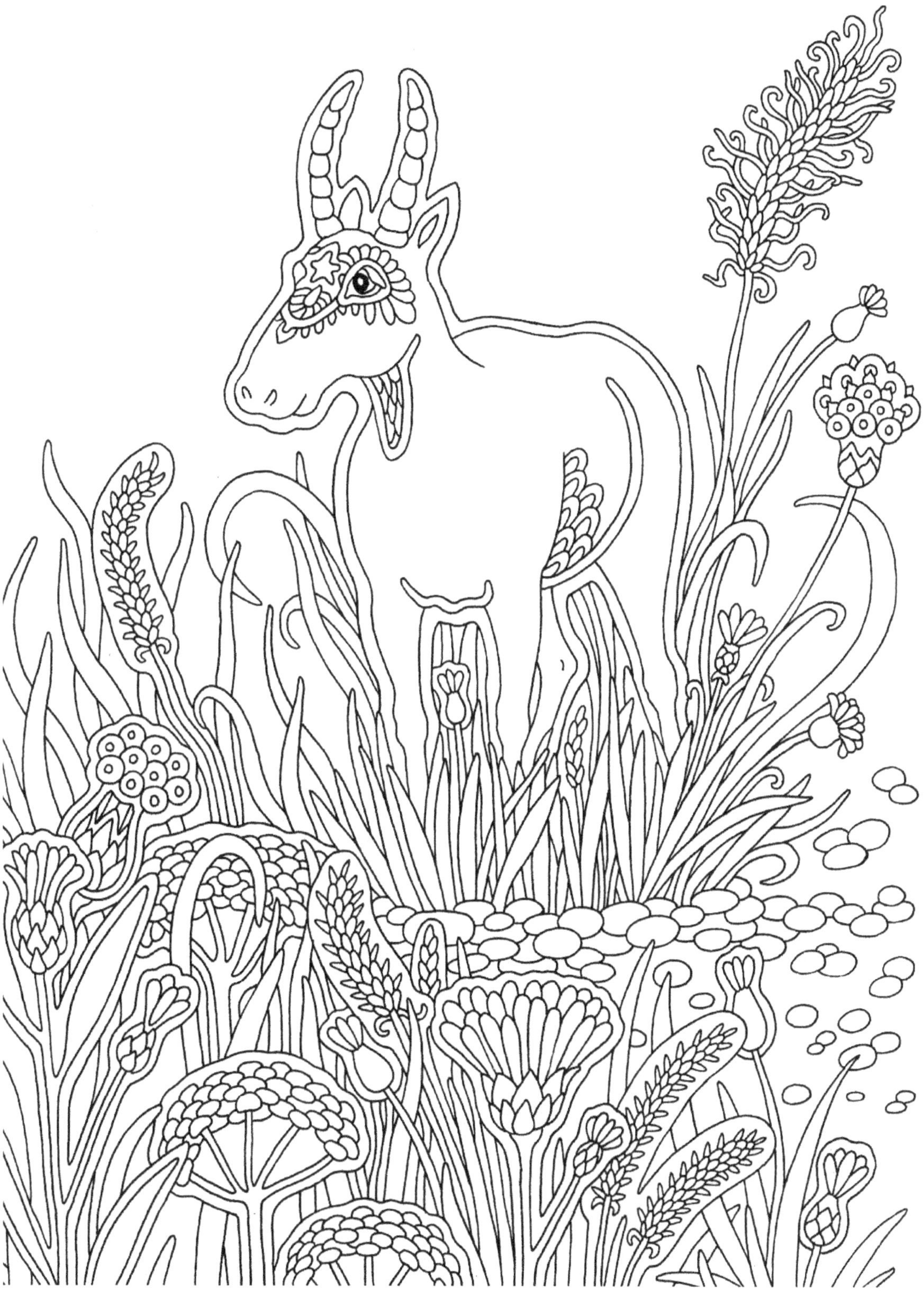

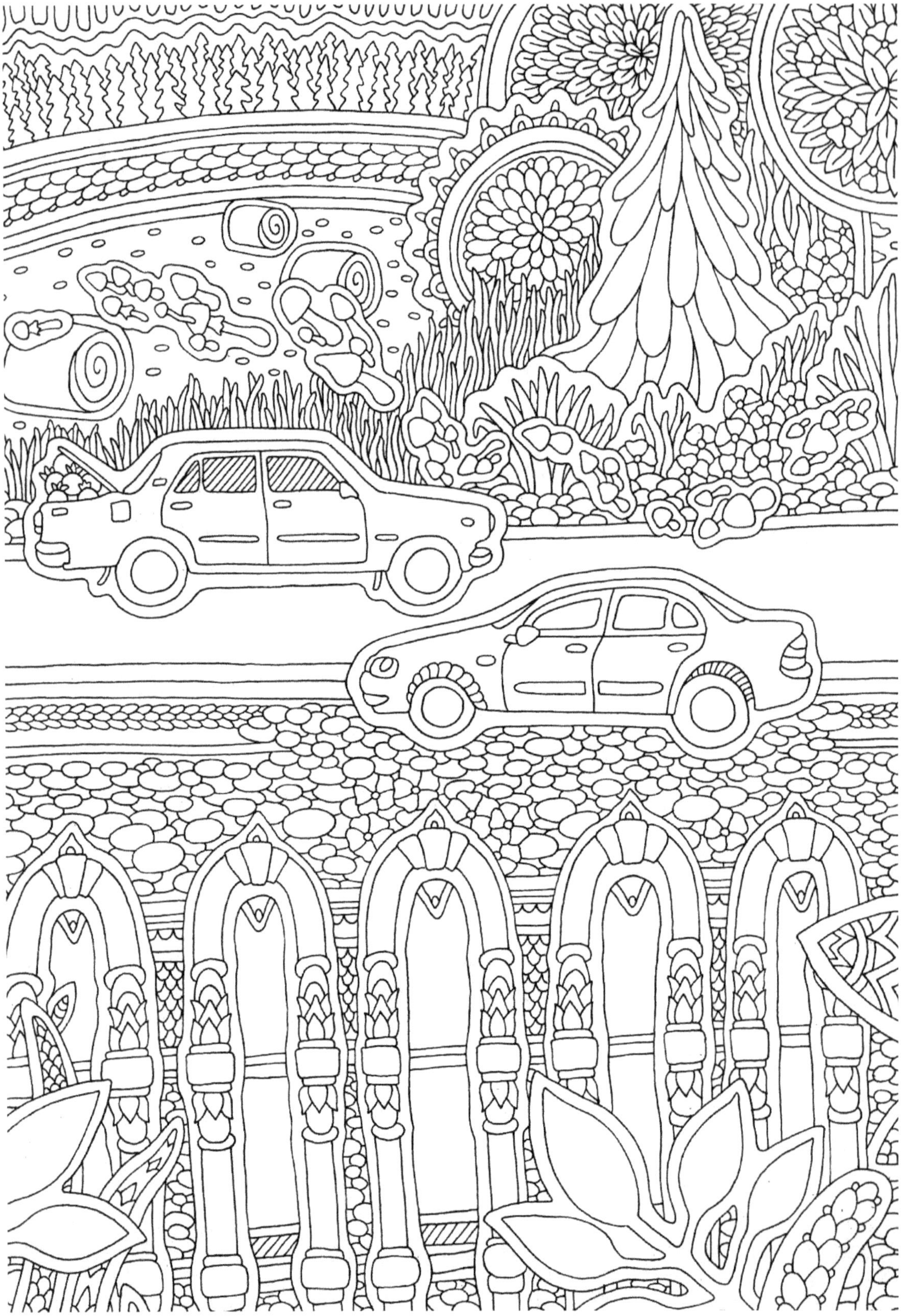

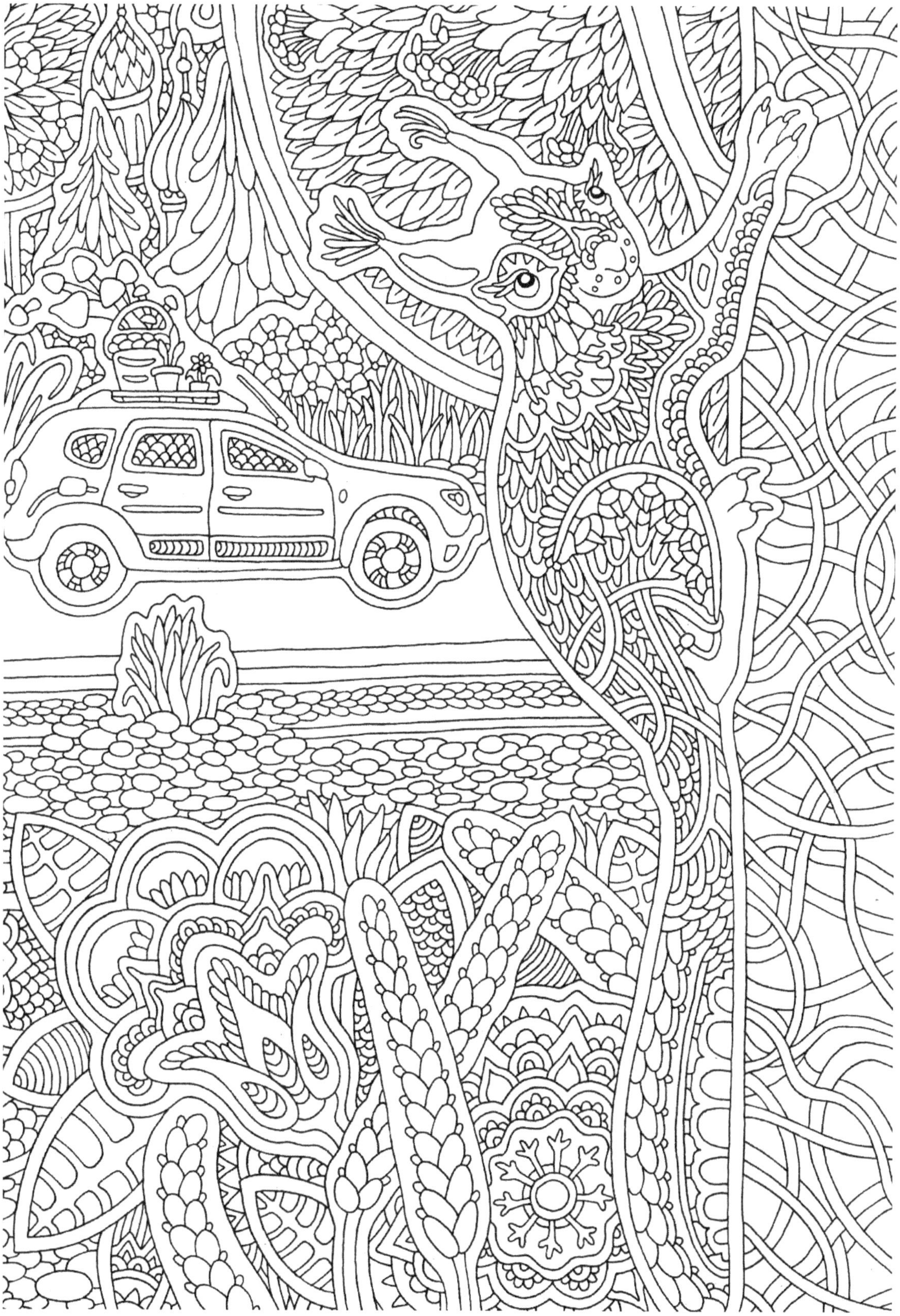

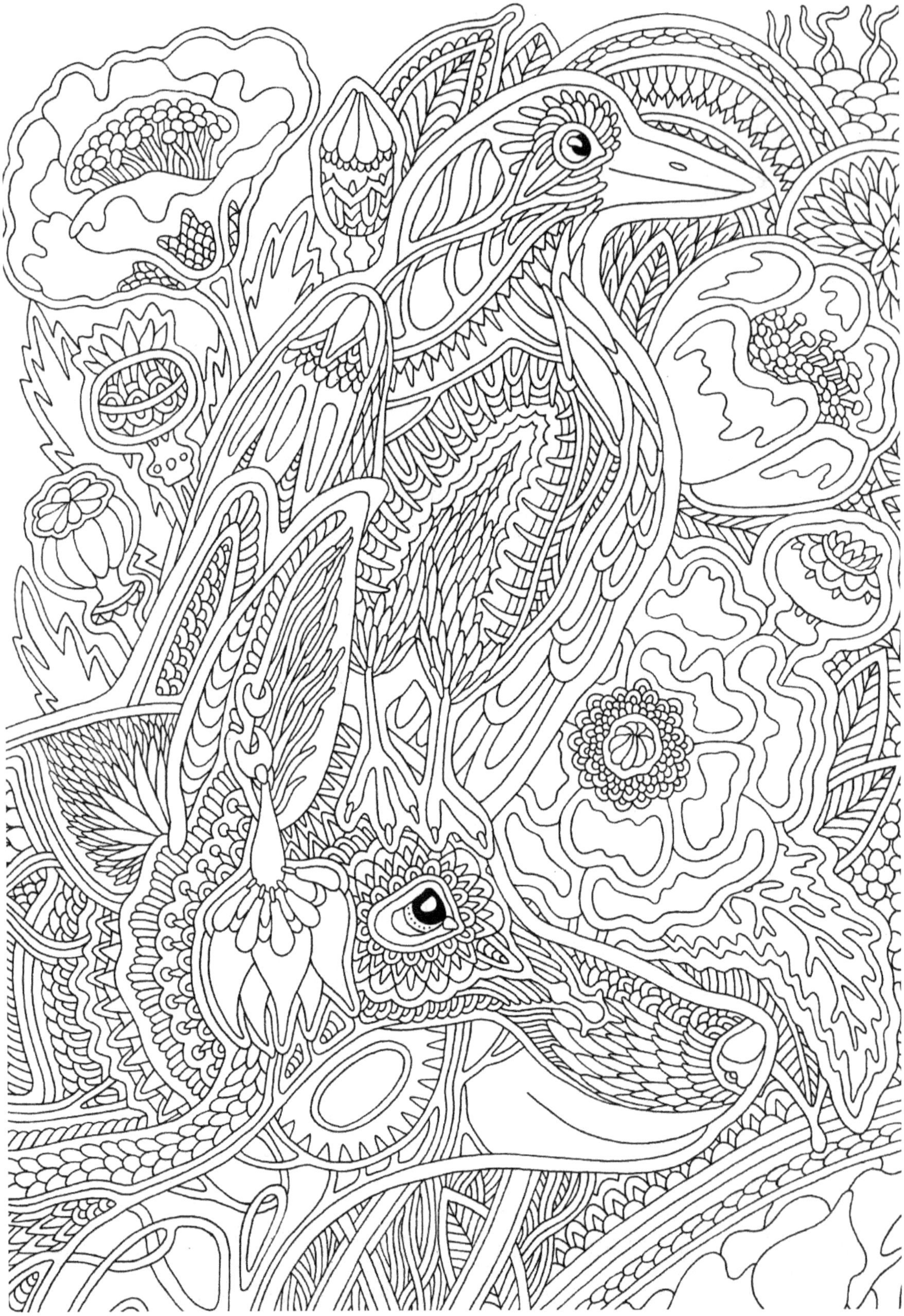

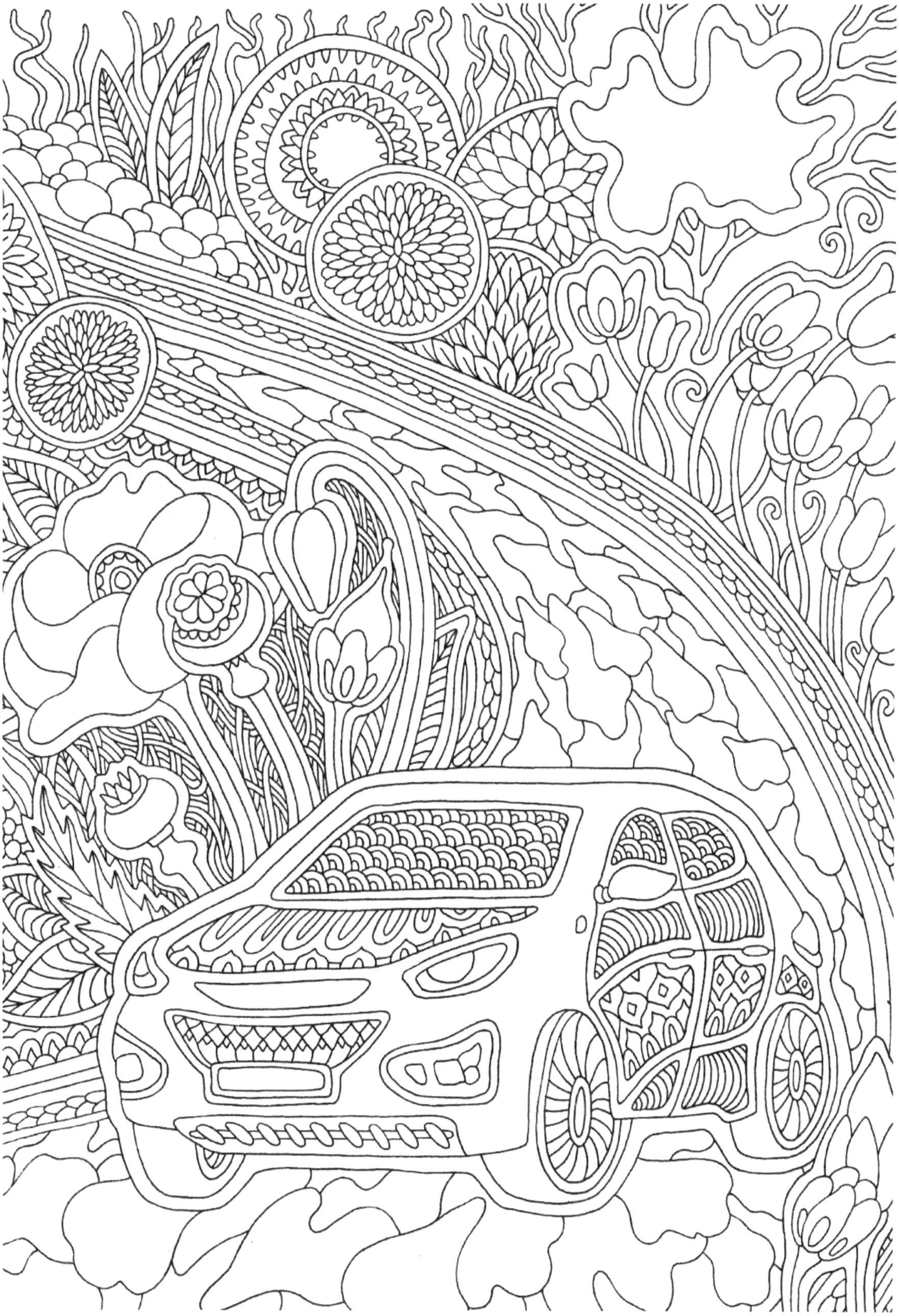

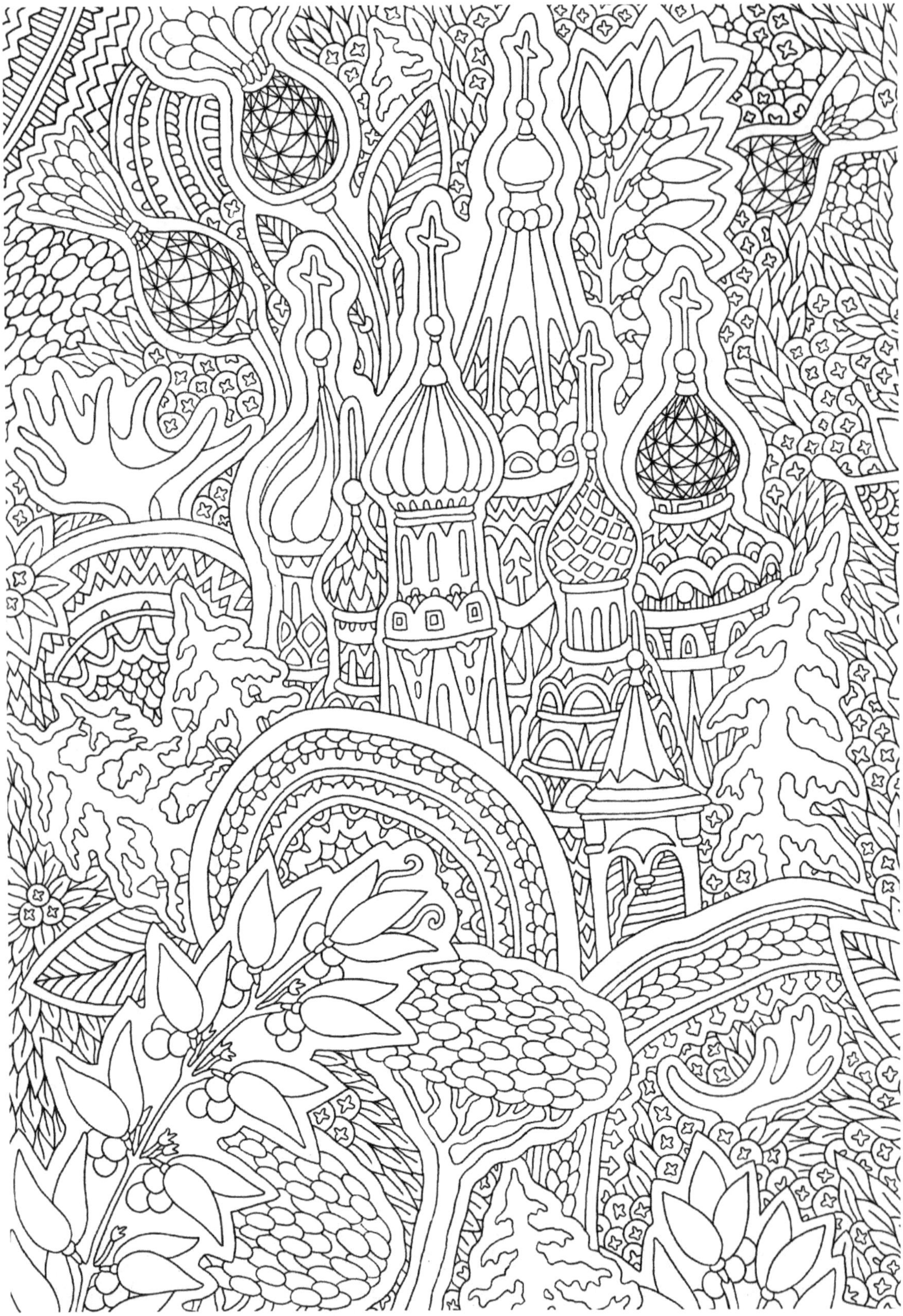

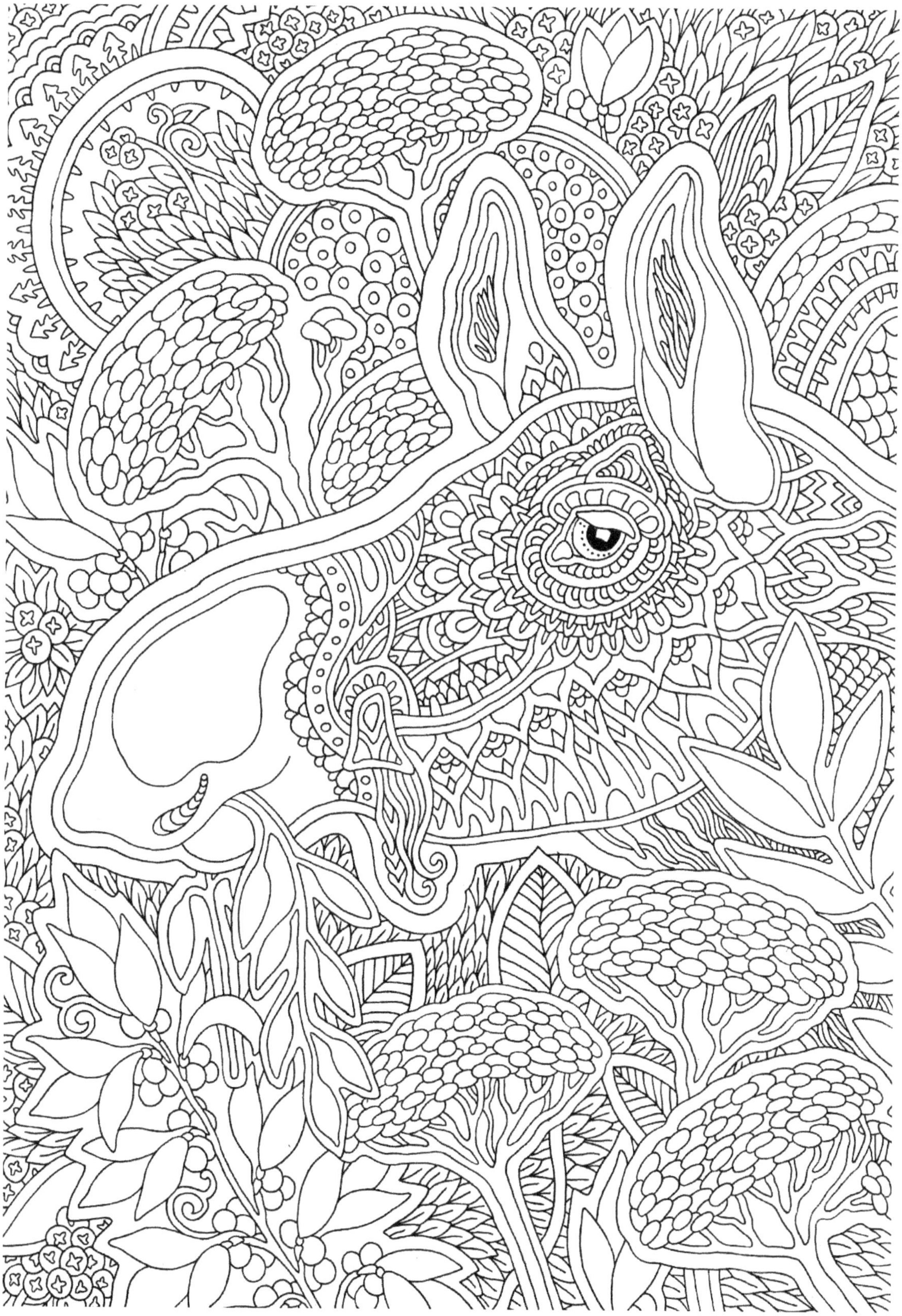

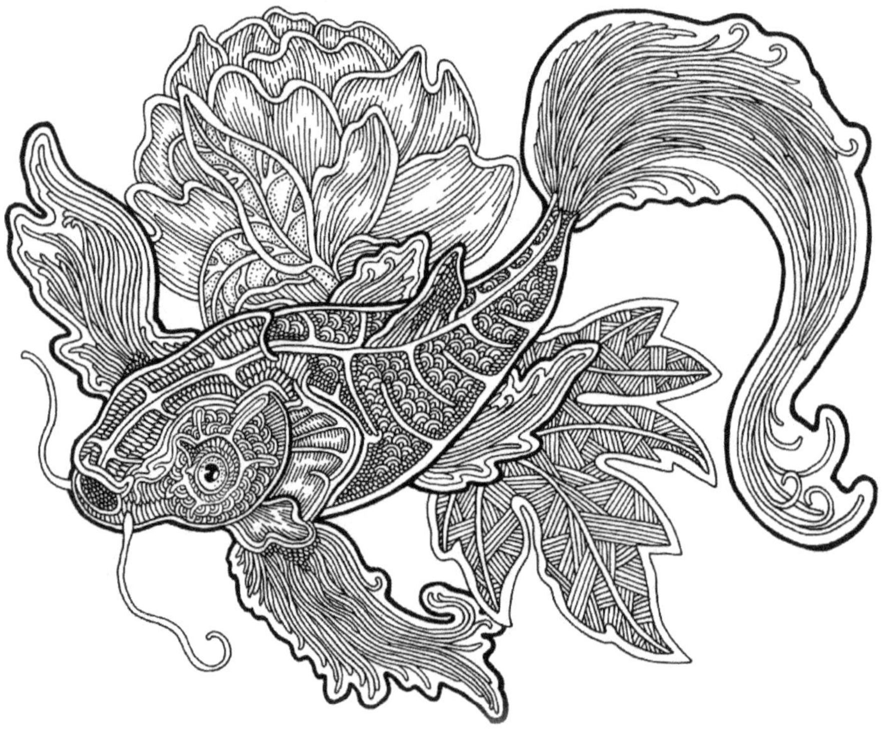

www.ingramcontent.com/pod-product-compliance
Lightning Source LLC
Chambersburg PA
CBHW080716190526
45169CB00006B/2393
* 9 7 8 1 5 3 3 4 2 1 7 8 4 *